RANDOM HOUSE
LARGE
PRINT

Build the Life You Want

Build the Life You Want

The Art and Science of Getting Happier

Arthur C. Brooks
and
Oprah Winfrey

Published in the United States of America by Random House Large Print in association with Portfolio / Penguin, an imprint of Penguin Random House LLC.

Cover design by Jennifer Heuer
Cover art: Lvqi Peng / iStock / Getty Images Plus

The Library of Congress has established a Cataloging-in-Publication record for this title.

ISBN: 978-0-593-79299-5

www.penguinrandomhouse.com/large-print-format-books

FIRST LARGE PRINT EDITION

Printed in the United States of America

1st Printing

We dedicate this book to you on your life's journey. May you get happier, year after year, and bring greater happiness to others.

Contents

Building What Matters

A Note from Oprah

One of the many things I got from doing **The Oprah Winfrey Show** for twenty-five years was a front-row seat to unhappiness. Of every, and I mean every, kind. My guests included people devastated by tragedy, or betrayal, or deep disappointment. Angry people and people who held grudges. People full of regret and guilt, shame and fear. People doing everything in their power to numb their unhappiness but waking up each day unhappy anyway.

I also witnessed abundant happiness. People who had found love and friendship. People using their talents and abilities to do good things. People who reaped the rewards of selflessness and giving, including one person who'd even donated a kidney to a stranger he'd recently met. People with a spiritual side that brought richer meaning to their lives. People who'd been given a second chance.

Where the audience was concerned, the unhappy guests generally provoked empathy; the happy ones, admiration (and maybe a twinge of wistful envy). And then there was a third category of guest that audiences didn't know **what** to make of but were genuinely inspired by: people who had every reason to be unhappy and yet were not. The lemonade-making, silver-linings-finding, bright-side-looking glass-half-fullers. The Mattie Stepaneks, is how I came to think of them—Mattie Stepanek being the boy who had a rare and fatal form of muscular dystrophy called dysautonomic mitochondrial myopathy, yet managed to find peace in all things and play after every storm. He wrote lovely poetry, was wise beyond his years, and was the first guest I ever befriended beyond the show. I used to call him my angel guy.

How could a boy with a fatal disease be as happy as Mattie was? Same with the mother who was full of peace and purpose and actual joy even as she was preparing to die, recording hundreds of voice tapes for her then-six-year-old daughter about how to live. And the Zimbabwean woman who was married at age eleven, beaten daily, yet instead of giving in to despair, maintained hope, set secret goals, and eventually achieved them—including earning a PhD.

How could these people even get out of bed in the morning, let alone be such rays of light? How did they do it? Were they born that way? Was there a secret or pattern of development the rest of the world should know? Because trust me, if there **was** such a thing, the world would definitely want to know. In my twenty-five years of doing the show, if there was one thing almost everyone in every audience had in common, it was the desire to be happy. As I've said before, after every show I'd chat with the audience, and I always asked what they most wanted in life. To be happy, they'd say. Just to be happy. Just happiness.

Except, as I've also said before, when I asked what happiness was, people suddenly weren't sure. They'd hem and haw and finally say "losing X number of pounds" or "having enough money to pay my bills" or "my kids—I just want my kids to be happy." So they had **goals,** or **wishes,** but they couldn't articulate what happiness looked like. Seldom did anyone have a real answer.

This book has the answer, because Arthur Brooks has studied and researched and lived the answer.

I first came across Arthur through his column in **The Atlantic,** "How to Build a Life." I started reading it during the pandemic and it quickly became something I looked forward to every week because it was all about what I've always cared most about: living a life with purpose and meaning. Then I read his book **From Strength to Strength,** a remarkable guide to becoming happier as you age. This man was singing my song.

Clearly, I had to talk to him. And when I did, I instantly realized that if I'd still been doing **The Oprah Winfrey Show,** I would have been calling on him all the time—he would have had something relevant and revealing to contribute to almost every topic we discussed. Arthur exudes a kind of confidence and certainty about the meaning of happiness that's both comforting and galvanizing. He's able to talk both broadly and very specifically about the very same things I've been talking about for years: how to grow into your best self, how to become a better human being. So I knew from the start that I would somehow end up working with him. That somehow is this book.

A Note from Arthur

"You must naturally be a very happy person."

I hear this all the time. It makes sense, after all: I teach courses on happiness at Harvard University. I write a regular happiness column for **The Atlantic.** I speak about the science of happiness all around the world. So, people assume, I must have natural gifts for happiness, like a professional basketball player must be a naturally gifted athlete. Lucky me, right?

But happiness isn't like basketball. You don't have a leg up on becoming a happiness specialist by being blessed with natural well-being. On the contrary, naturally happy people almost never study happiness, because to them, it doesn't seem like something one needs to study, or even think much about. It would be like studying air.

The truth is that I write, speak, and teach about happiness precisely because it's naturally hard for me, and I want more of it. My baseline well-being level—the level where I would sit if I didn't study it and work on it every day—is significantly lower than average. It's not as if I have had huge trauma or unusual suffering. No one should feel sorry for me. It just runs in the family: my grandfather was gloomy; my father was anxious; left to my own devices, I am gloomy and anxious. Just ask my wife of thirty-two years, Ester. (She's nodding **yes** as she reads this.) So my work as a social scientist isn't research—it's **me**-search.

If you are coming to this book because you are not as happy as you want to be—whether because you are suffering from something in particular, or you have a good life "on paper" but always find yourself struggling—you are the kind of person I relate to best. We are kindred spirits.

When I started studying happiness twenty-five years ago as a PhD student, I didn't know if academic knowledge would help. I feared that happiness wasn't something you could change in a meaningful way. Maybe it was like astronomy, I thought. You can learn about the stars, but you can't change them. And in fact, for a long time, my knowledge didn't help me very much. I knew a lot, but it wasn't practical in any way. It was just observations about who the happiest people were—and the unhappiest.

A decade ago during a particularly dark and stormy time in my life, Ester asked a question that changed my thinking. "Why don't you use all that complicated research to see if there are ways you can change your own habits?" Obvious, right? For some reason, it wasn't obvious to me at all, but I was willing to try. I started spending more time observing my well-being levels to pick out patterns. I studied the nature of my suffering and the benefits I likely derived from it. I set up a series of experiments based on the data, trying things like making a gratitude list, praying more, and pursuing the opposite behavior of my inclination when I was sad and angry (which was pretty often).

And I saw results. As a matter of fact, it worked so well that in my spare time from my job running a large nonprofit organization, I started writing about happiness and real-life applications in **The New York Times** to share them with others. People began to get in touch to say the science of happiness—translated into practical advice—was helping them, too. And I found that teaching ideas in this way solidified the knowledge in my mind and made me even happier.

Obviously, I wanted more. So I changed careers. At the age of fifty-five, I quit my chief executive job, with a plan to write, speak, and teach about the science of happiness. I started by creating a simple personal mission statement for myself.

> I dedicate my work to lifting people up and bringing them together, in bonds of love and happiness, using science and ideas.

I accepted a professorship at Harvard University and created a class on the science of happiness, which quickly became oversubscribed. Then I started a regular column on the subject at **The Atlantic** that found a readership of hundreds of thousands a week. I investigated a new happiness topic every week by using my background as a quantitative researcher to read the cutting-edge psychology, neuroscience, economics, and philosophy. Then I turned the learnings into real-life experiments on myself. When it worked, I would teach my students what I learned, and publish it publicly for a mass audience.

As the years turned over, I saw more and more progress in my life. I observed how my brain was processing negative emotions and learned how to manage these emotions without trying to get rid of them. I began to see relationships as an interplay between hearts and brains, and not some inscrutable mystery. I started adopting the habits of the happiest people that I saw in the data, and whom I knew in my real life (including someone very special, whom you will meet in the Introduction that comes next). At the same time, I began to hear from people all around the world—some I had never heard of, others very famous—who were learning with me that they could raise their own happiness levels if they did the work to learn and apply their knowledge.

In the years since I made this life change, my own well-being has risen **a lot.** People notice and remark that I smile more, and I look like I'm having more fun in my work. My relationships are better than they were. And I have seen improvements like this in students, business leaders, and ordinary people who learn the principles. Many of them have experienced pain and loss beyond anything I have ever faced, and found joy even amid their suffering.

I still have plenty of bad days, and I have a long way to go, but today I am comfortable with my bad days, and I know how to grow from them. I know rough times will come, but I'm not afraid of them. And I am confident that there is a lot of progress in my future.

Sometimes I think back to myself at thirty-five or forty-five years old, when I was so rarely joyful and looked to the future with a sense of resignation. If fifty-nine-year-old me went back in time and said, "You are going to learn to be happier, and teach the secrets to others," I probably would have said that future me had gone insane. But it's true (the getting happier part—not the going insane part).

And now I am privileged to team up in my work with someone I have admired since I was a young man—a person who herself has lifted up millions of people in bonds of love and happiness all over the world: Oprah Winfrey. When we first met, we quickly realized that we shared a mission, even though we pursued it in different ways—I in academia, and Oprah in mass media.

Our mission in this book is to tie together the two strands of our work, to open up the amazing science of happiness to people in all walks of life, who can use it to live better and lift up others. In plain language, we seek to help you see that you are not helpless against the tides of life, but that with a greater understanding of how your mind and brain work, you can build the life you want, starting inside with your emotions, and then turning outward to your family, friendships, work, and spiritual life.

It worked for us, and it can work for you, too.

Introduction

Albina's Secret

From Arthur: Albina Quevedo, my mother-in-law, whom I loved like my own mother, lay in her bed in the small Barcelona apartment she had occupied for the past seventy years. The bedroom's austere decor had never changed: a picture on one wall of her native Canary Islands; a simple crucifix on another. This was what she saw nearly twenty-four hours a day, since a fall two years earlier had left her in pain and unable to get up or walk by herself. At ninety-three, she knew she was in her last months.

Her body was weak, but her mind was still sharp and her memories vivid. She talked about decades past, times when she was youthful, healthy, newly married, and starting her beloved family. She reminisced about parties and days at the beach with close friends, now long dead. She laughed as she remembered those good times.

"Such a difference with my life now," she said.

She turned her head on the pillow and looked out the window for a long time, lost in thought. Turning back, she said, "I am much happier than I was back then."

She looked over at my surprised face, and explained. "I know it sounds strange because my life now seems bleak, but it's true," she said with a smile. "As I've aged, I have learned the secret to getting happier."

I was all ears now.

As I sat at her bedside, Albina recounted the trials of her life. As a little girl in the 1930s, she had lived through the brutal Spanish Civil War, some of it in hiding, often going hungry and seeing death and suffering all around her. Her father was arrested and spent years in prison for serving on the losing side of that conflict as a battlefield surgeon. Despite that, she always saw her childhood as a happy one, because her parents loved her and loved each other, and this love was the memory that endured most clearly. And speaking of love, the man in the prison cell next to her father's introduced her to her future husband.

So far, so good. But that's when trouble started for Albina. After a few good years and the births of three children, her husband turned out to be less than stellar, abandoning her without child support and plunging them into poverty. Her sadness over being deserted was compounded by the pressures of raising kids alone, while sometimes wondering if she could keep the lights on.

For several years, she felt stuck and miserable, concluding that a happier life was unavailable as long as the world dealt her this very bad hand. Almost every day, she would look out the front window of her small apartment and cry.

Who could blame her? Her poverty and loneliness, which made her miserable, were not of her doing—they had been imposed on her, and she couldn't see a way to change them. As long as her circumstances didn't change, her unhappiness would persist, and a better life seemed impossible.

One day, when Albina was forty-five, something changed for her. For reasons that were not clear to her friends and family, her outlook on life seemed to shift. It's not that she was suddenly less lonely, or that she mysteriously came into money, but for some reason, she stopped waiting for the world to change and took control of her life.

The most obvious change she made was to enroll in college to become a teacher. It wasn't easy. Studying day and night alongside students half her age, while raising a family, was completely exhausting, but it was a life-changing success. At the end of three years Albina finished college at the top of her class.

She now embarked on a new career she loved,

teaching in an economically marginalized neighborhood where she served children and families in poverty. She truly became her own person, was able to support her own kids with her own money, and made friends she would cherish and who would be by her side until her last days—and who would openly weep at her funeral.

More than a decade later, Albina's wayward husband wanted to return; they had never formally divorced. She considered it and took him back—not because she needed to, but because she wanted to. Her husband found Albina completely changed in his fourteen years away: she was stronger and, well, happier. They never separated again, and in their later years, he was a different person as well, caring for her lovingly. He had died three years earlier.

"We were happily married for fifty-four years," she said. Then, clarifying with a smile: "Technically, that's sixty-eight years married, minus the fourteen unhappy ones."

Now here she was at age ninety-three, with her circumstances once again limiting her, but her joy undiminished—and even increasing. I wasn't the only one who noticed; everyone marveled at the way her happiness grew as she aged.

What was her secret to turning the corner at forty-five toward a better life—and getting happier for nearly five decades after that?

THE SECRET

Some people might dismiss Albina's story by saying that she was a rare person with a natural gift for making lemonade out of lemons. But her perspective on life wasn't innate; it was learned and cultivated. She wasn't just "naturally happy." On the contrary, by her own account, she was quite unhappy for a long time before her big change.

Or one might say she was just really good at "whistling past the graveyard"—ignoring the bad things in life. But that's not true, either. She never denied that bad things had happened, or pretended she wasn't suffering now. She knew full well that getting old was going to be hard; that losing friends and loved ones was going to be sad; that being sick would be scary and painful. She didn't get happier by blocking out those realities.

Something happened that changed Albina and set her free. Three things, actually.

First, one day in her midforties, a simple thought occurred to her. She had always believed that getting happier required the outside world to change. After all, her problems came from outside—from bad luck and the behavior of others. This was comfortable in a way, but it left her in a kind of suspended animation.

Just maybe, she thought, even if she couldn't change her circumstances, she could change her own **reaction** to those circumstances. She couldn't decide how the world would treat her, but maybe she had some say in how she would feel about it. Maybe she didn't have to wait for the difficulty or suffering in her life to diminish to start getting on with business.

She began to look for decisions in her life where once there were only impositions. The despairing hopelessness of feeling herself to be at the mercy of her estranged husband, of the economy, of the needs of her children, began to subside. Her circumstances weren't the boss of how she felt about life—she was.

Up to that point, Albina said, she had felt like she was stuck in a bad job at a terrible company. Now she had awakened to realize that she had been the CEO all along. That didn't mean she could snap her fingers and make everything perfect—CEOs suffer in bad times, too—but it did mean she had a lot of power over her own life, and it could lead to all sorts of good things down the line.

Further, Albina took action based on that realization. She switched from wishing others were different to working on the one person she could control: herself. She felt negative emotions just like anyone else, but she set about making more conscious choices about how to react to them. The decisions she made—not her primal feelings—led her to try to transform less productive emotions into positive ones such as gratitude, hope, compassion, and humor. She also worked to focus more on the world around her and less on her own problems. None of this was easy, but she got better at it with practice, and it felt more and more natural as the weeks and months went by.

Finally, managing herself freed Albina to focus on the pillars on which she could construct a much better life: her family, her friendships, her work, and her faith. Successfully managing herself, Albina was no longer distracted by life's constant crises. No longer managed by her feelings, she chose a relationship with her husband that didn't deny the past, but that worked. She built a loving bond with her children. She cultivated deep personal friendships. She found a career that gave her a sense of service and earned success. She walked her own spiritual path. And she taught others how to live this way, too.

In these three steps, Albina built the life she wanted.

THE ROAD AHEAD

If you can relate to Albina's plight, or if you feel a need to improve your happiness for other reasons, you are not alone. America is in a happiness slump. Just over the past decade, the percentage of Americans saying they are "not too happy" rose from 10 percent to 24 percent.[1] The percentage of Americans suffering from depression is increasing dramatically, especially among young adults.[2]

Meanwhile, the percentage saying they are "very happy" has fallen from 36 percent to 19 percent.[3] These patterns are seen all over the globe, too, and the trend existed even before the COVID-19 pandemic started.[4] People disagree about why this slump is happening on such a mass scale—blaming technology, or a polarized culture, or culture change, or the economy, or even politics—but we all know that it is happening.

Most of us don't have the ambition of pulling the whole world out of the slump; we'd be content to help just ourselves. But how, when our problems come from the outside? If we're angry or sad or lonely, we need people to treat us better; we need our finances to improve; we need our luck to change. Until then, we wait, unhappily, and can only distract ourselves from discomfort.

This book is about showing you how to break out of this pattern, like Albina did. You, too, can become the boss of your own life, not an observer. You can learn to choose how you react to negative circumstances and select emotions that make you happier even when you get a bad hand. You can focus your energy not on trivial distractions, but on the basic pillars of happiness that bring enduring satisfaction and meaning.

You will learn how to manage your life in new ways. However, unlike other books you may have read (we've read them, too), this one is not going to exhort you to pull yourself up by your bootstraps.

This isn't a book about willpower—it's about knowledge, and how to use it. If you couldn't figure out something about your car, you wouldn't solve the problem with extreme willpower—you'd look at an owner's manual. Similarly, when something isn't right in your happiness, you need clear, science-based information about how your happiness works before anything else, and then instructions on how to use this information in your life. That's what this book is.

This also isn't another book about minimizing or eliminating pain—yours or anyone else's. Life can be hard—much harder for some people than for others, through no fault of their own. If you're in pain, this book won't tell you to wait it out or extinguish it. Rather, it will show you how to decide to deal with it, learn from it, and grow through it.

Finally, this book isn't any kind of quick fix for your life. For Albina, getting happier took effort and patience, and it will for you, too. Reading this book is just the start. Practicing the skills requires, well, practice. Some progress will be immediate, and most likely, people around you will notice positive changes (and ask your advice). Other lessons will take months or years to become internal and automatic. That's not bad news at all, because the process of managing yourself and making progress is a fun adventure. Getting happier becomes a new way of life.

Building the life you want takes time and effort.

To delay means waiting for no good reason, missing more time being happier, and making others happier as well. Albina was unwilling to do that—she was unwilling to miss the life she wanted while waiting for the universe to change.

If you, too, are done waiting, let's get started.

Build the Life You Want

One

Happiness Is Not the Goal, and Unhappiness Is Not the Enemy

The professor grinned from ear to ear as he addressed the packed auditorium at Carnegie Mellon University in Pittsburgh on a September evening in 2007. It was his last lecture there, and he was ebullient with joy as he looked back on his life's work, on finding good in others, overcoming obstacles, and living with passion. He was so filled with energy and vigor that he could barely contain himself. At one point, he dropped to the floor and performed a set of one-armed push-ups.[1]

The professor was Randy Pausch, a well-known computer scientist, beloved by his students and colleagues at Carnegie Mellon. You might think that his joy at his last lecture was because he was retiring to the Caribbean, or perhaps more likely (he was just forty-seven) moving to a plum post elsewhere. Neither of these things was true, though.

It was his last lecture because Professor Pausch had terminal pancreatic cancer, and had been given just a few months to live.

The audience came to hear him, not sure what to expect. Would it be a tragic reflection on the shortness of life? A list of should-haves? To be sure, there were a great deal of tears in the auditorium that night, but not from Randy. "If I don't seem as depressed or morose as I should be," he wisecracked, "sorry to disappoint you." His speech was a celebration of life, full of love and joy, to be shared with friends, coworkers, his wife, and his three young children.

There was simply no denying that Randy was a man who enjoyed a huge amount of happiness. Even his grim diagnosis could not suppress that self-evident truth that September night. Over the next few months, as his health permitted, he enjoyed life to its fullest, inspiring others through the national media (including Oprah's show) and posting to his personal web page the details of his health and treatments, as well as family milestones and many moments of personal joy.

On July 25, 2008, Randy Pausch died, surrounded by his family and friends.

In his final months, Randy had done something most of us would consider unthinkable: he had spent what would naturally be the hardest, gloomiest part of his life getting happier. How did he do that?

TWO MYTHS ABOUT HAPPINESS

There's nothing strange about wanting to be happy. "There is no one who does not wish to be happy,"[2] the theologian and philosopher Augustine flatly declared in 426 CE, with absolutely no evidence necessary then or now. Find us someone who says, "I don't care about being happy," and we will show you someone either delusional or not telling the truth.

What do people mean when they say they "want to be happy"? Usually, two things: First, they are saying they want to achieve (and keep) certain feelings—joyfulness, cheerfulness, or something similar. Second, they are saying there is some obstacle to getting this feeling. "I want to be happy" is almost always followed by "but . . ."

Consider Claudia, an office manager in New York. At age thirty-five, she's been living with her boyfriend for the past five years. They love each other, but he is not ready to make a permanent commitment. Claudia doesn't feel that she can plan for the future—where she will live, whether she will have kids, how her career arc will go. This frustrates her and leaves her at loose ends, making her feel sad and angry. She wants to be happy, but doesn't think she can be until her boyfriend makes up his mind.

Or consider Ryan. He thought that when he was in college he would make lifelong friends and set his career goals. Instead, he came out of school more confused about life than when he went in. Now, at age twenty-five, he's thousands of dollars in debt, jumps from job to job, and feels aimless. He hopes he will be happy when the right opportunity comes along and makes his future clear.

Margaret is fifty. Ten years ago, she thought she had everything figured out—she worked part-time, her kids were in high school, and she was active in her community. But since her children left the nest, she's felt restless and dissatisfied with everything. She browses houses on Zillow, thinking it might be helpful to move. She thinks a big change will bring happiness, but she doesn't know what the necessary change is.

Finally, there's Ted. Since he retired, he hasn't had real friends. He's lost touch with everyone from work. He's been divorced for years, and his adult children are focused on their own families. Sometimes he reads, but he mostly watches television to pass the time. He thinks he would be happy if there were more people in his life, but he can't seem to find them.

Claudia, Ryan, Margaret, and Ted are normal people with normal problems—nothing strange or scandalous. (They're actually composites of people whom we have met and worked with many times.) Each is dealing with the ordinary difficulties that any of us could face in our lives, even without making big missteps or taking foolish risks. And their beliefs about happiness and life are normal—but mistaken.

Claudia, Ryan, Margaret, and Ted all are living in a state of "I want to be happy, but . . ." If you break that down, you'll see that it's predicated on two beliefs:

1. I can be happy . . .
2. . . . but my circumstances are keeping me stuck in unhappiness.

The truth is that both those beliefs, as persuasive as they sound, are false. You can't be happy—though you **can** be happier. And your circumstances and your source of unhappiness **don't** have to stop you.

Here's what we mean when we say you can't be happy. Searching for happiness is like searching for El Dorado, the fabled South American city of gold no one has ever found. When we search for happiness, we may get glimpses of what it might feel like, but it doesn't last. People talk about it, and some claim to possess it, but the people who society says should be completely happy—the rich, the beautiful, the famous, the powerful—often seem to wind up in the news with their bankruptcies, personal scandals, and family troubles. Some people do have more happiness than others, but no one can master it consistently.

If the secret to total happiness existed, we would have all found it by now. It would be big business, sold on the internet, taught in every school, and probably provided by the government. But it isn't. That's kind of weird, isn't it? The one thing we all want, since **Homo sapiens** appeared three hundred thousand years ago in Africa, has remained elusive to pretty much everybody. We've figured out how to make fire, the wheel, the lunar lander, and TikTok videos, but with all that human ingenuity, we have not mastered the art and science of getting and keeping the one thing we **really** want.

That's because happiness is not a destination. Happiness is a **direction.** We won't find complete happiness on this side of heaven, but no matter where each of us is in life, we can all be **happier.** And then happier, and then happier still.

The fact that complete happiness in this life is impossible might seem like disappointing news, but it isn't. It's the best news ever, actually. It means we all can finally stop looking for the lost city that doesn't exist, once and for all. We can stop wondering what's wrong with us because we can't find or keep it.

We can also stop believing that our individual problems are the reasons we haven't achieved happiness. No positive circumstance can give us the state of bliss we seek. But no negative circumstance can make getting happier impossible, either. Here is a fact: You can get happier, even if you have problems.

You can even get happier in some cases **because** you have problems.

These two mistaken beliefs, and not what life throws at us, are the real reason so many people are stuck and miserable. They want something that doesn't exist, and they think that any progress is impossible until all the barriers in life are cleared away. And these errors start with an incorrect answer to a very innocent-sounding question: **What is happiness?**

WHAT IS HAPPINESS?

Imagine you asked somebody to define a car. She thinks about your question, and then answers, "A car is . . . well, it's the feeling I get when I am in a chair, but like a chair that I sit in when I want to get groceries." You would assume she really doesn't know what a car is. And you certainly won't lend her the keys to **yours.**

Then, you ask her to define a boat. She thinks for a minute and says, "It's not a car."

This is an absurd scenario. And yet weirdly, these are the kinds of definitions we usually get when we ask someone to define happiness and unhappiness. Try it yourself. You'll get something like, "Happiness is . . . well, I guess it's a feeling . . . like when I'm with people I love or I'm doing something I enjoy." And unhappiness? "It's the lack of happiness."

The biggest reason people don't get happier is because they don't even know what they are trying to increase. And the reason they feel stuck in their unhappiness is because they can't define what it is. If this is your predicament, don't feel too bad. Most people struggle with these definitions. They talk about feelings, or use bland metaphors, like "sunshine in my soul," which an old Presbyterian hymn called happiness.[3]

Even the ancient philosophers struggled to agree on the definition of happiness. For example, consider the battle between Epicurus and Epictetus.

Epicurus (341–270 BCE) led a school of thought named after himself—Epicureanism—that argued that a happy life requires two things: ataraxia (freedom from mental disturbance) and aponia (the absence of physical pain). His philosophy might be characterized as "If it is scary or painful, avoid it." Epicureans saw discomfort as generally negative, and thus the elimination of threats and problems as the key to a happier life. Not that they were lazy or unmotivated. They didn't see enduring fear and pain as inherently necessary or beneficial, and they focused instead on enjoying life.

Epictetus lived about three hundred years after Epicurus and was one of the most prominent Stoic philosophers. He believed happiness comes from finding life's purpose, accepting one's fate, and behaving morally regardless of the personal cost—and he didn't think much of Epicurus's feel-good beliefs. His philosophy could be summarized as "Grow a spine and do your duty." People who followed a Stoic style saw happiness as something earned through a good deal of sacrifice. Not surprisingly, Stoics were generally hard workers who lived for the future and were willing to incur substantial personal cost to meet their life's purpose (as they saw it) without much complaining. They saw the key to happiness as accepting pain and fear, not actively avoiding them.

Today, people still break down along Epicurean and Stoic lines—they look for happiness either in feeling good or in doing their duty. And the definitions only multiply from there, especially as we travel around the world. Take, for example, the differences scholars find between Western and Eastern cultures.[4] In the West, happiness is usually defined in terms of excitement and achievement. Meanwhile, in Asia, happiness is most often defined in terms of calm and contentment.

Definitions of happiness even depend on the word for it. In Germanic languages, **happiness** is rooted in words related to fortune or positive fate.[5] In fact, **happiness** comes from the Old Norse **happ,** which means "luck."[6] Meanwhile, in Latin-based languages, the term comes from **felicitas,** which referred in ancient Rome not just to good luck but also to growth, fertility, and prosperity.[7] Other languages have special words just for the subject. Danes often describe happiness in terms of **hygge,** which is something like coziness and comfortable conviviality.[8]

If happiness were really this subjective—or even worse, a matter of feelings at any given moment—there would be no way to study it. It would be like trying to nail Jell-O to the wall. This book would be two words long: **good luck** (or maybe good **happ**).

Fortunately, we can do a lot better than this today. It's true that different cultures define happiness somewhat differently, which is why the happiness comparisons among countries you always see in the news are not very useful or convincing. It is also true that feelings are associated with happiness. Your emotions affect how happy you are, and how happy you are affects all your emotions. But this doesn't mean that there are no constants across all people, or that happiness **is** a feeling.

A good way to define happiness is in terms of its component parts. If you had to define your Thanksgiving dinner, you might do so by listing the dishes—turkey, stuffing, sweet potatoes, and so on. Or you might list the ingredients, if you are a good cook. Or, if you are kind of a nutrition buff, you might say that dinner—all food, actually—is made of its three macronutrients: carbohydrates, protein, and fat. To make a good and healthy dinner, you need all three of these in proper balance.

The dinner would also have a delicious smell that fills the house. Yet you wouldn't say that this smell

is the dinner. Rather, the smell is **evidence** of the dinner. And similarly, happy feelings are not happiness; they are evidence of happiness. The happiness itself is the real phenomenon, and like the dinner, it can be defined as a combination of three "macronutrients," which you need in balance and abundance in your life.

The macronutrients of happiness are enjoyment, satisfaction, and purpose.

The first is **enjoyment.** This might sound like pleasure—"feeling good." However, this isn't correct. Pleasure is animal; enjoyment is completely human. Pleasure emanates from parts of the brain dedicated to rewarding us for certain activities, like eating and sex, that in earlier times would help keep us alive and passing on our genes. (Today the things that bring pleasure—from substances to behaviors—are often maladapted and misused, leading to all sorts of problems.)

Enjoyment takes an urge for pleasure and adds two important things: communion and consciousness. For example, Thanksgiving dinner can bring pleasure when it tastes good and fills your belly, but it brings enjoyment when you eat with loved ones and make a warm memory together, employing the more conscious parts of your brain. Pleasure is easier than enjoyment, but it is a mistake to settle for it, because it is fleeting and solitary. All addictions involve pleasure, not enjoyment.

To be happier, you should never settle for pleasure,

but rather make it into enjoyment. Of course, that involves a certain cost. Enjoyment requires an investment of time and effort. It means forgoing an easy, effortless thrill. It often means saying no to cravings and temptations. Sometimes, getting enjoyment is hard.

The second macronutrient of happiness is **satisfaction.** It's that thrill from accomplishing a goal you worked for. It's that feeling you have when you get an A in school or a promotion at work; when you finally buy a house or get married. It's how you feel when you do something difficult—maybe even painful—that meets your life's purpose as you see it.

Satisfaction is wonderful, but it doesn't come without work and sacrifice. If you don't suffer for something—at least a little—it doesn't satisfy at all. If you study all week for a test and get a good grade, it gives you a lot of satisfaction. But if you cheat to get the same grade, in addition to doing the wrong thing, you probably get no satisfaction at all. This is one of the reasons why cutting corners in life is such a bad strategy—it ruins your ability to feel satisfied.

While satisfaction can bring a huge amount of joy, it is also extremely elusive: you think that meeting a goal will give you permanent satisfaction, but it is, of course, temporary. We all know the Rolling Stones' 1965 megahit "(I Can't Get No) Satisfaction." It's actually not right: you **can** get satisfaction; you just can't **keep** no satisfaction. It is incredibly frustrating—painful, even—that we strive like crazy, and as soon as we get that burst of joy, it's ripped away. That's why, as Jagger sings, we try, and we try, and we try to keep it, a behavior that psychologists call the hedonic treadmill, in which we adapt quickly to good things and have to keep running and running to keep feeling satisfaction.[9] This is especially true with worldly things like money, power, pleasure, and prestige (or fame).

The third macronutrient is the most important: **purpose.** We can make do without enjoyment for a while, and even without a lot of satisfaction. Without purpose, however, we are utterly lost, because we can't deal with life's inevitable puzzles and dilemmas. When we do have a sense of meaning and purpose, we can face life with hope and inner peace.

And yet, people who have a strong sense of meaning often find it in their suffering. That is the argument of psychiatrist and Holocaust survivor Viktor Frankl, whom we will meet in the next chapter. In his classic memoir, **Man's Search for Meaning,** he writes, "The way in which a man accepts his fate and all the suffering it entails, the way in which he takes up his cross, gives him ample opportunity—even under the most difficult circumstances—to add a deeper meaning to his life."[10] The common strategy of trying to eliminate suffering from life to get happier is futile and mistaken; we must instead look for the why of life to make pain an opportunity for growth.

THE ROLE OF UNHAPPINESS

Happiness is a combination of enjoyment, satisfaction, and purpose. To get happier is to get more of these elements, in a balanced way—not all of one and none of another. But if you were reading closely, you noticed one funny thing about all three: **they all have some unhappiness within them.** Enjoyment takes work and forgoing pleasures; satisfaction requires sacrifice and doesn't last; purpose almost always entails suffering. Getting happier, in other words, requires that we accept unhappiness in our lives as well, and understanding it isn't an obstacle to our happiness.

If you think this sounds counterintuitive, you're not alone. Until well into the twentieth century, unhappiness was generally seen as the lack of happiness, just like light and dark. Positive and negative emotions were seen by psychologists as existing on a continuum. For example, if you felt "less bad" as time passed after a loss or trauma, that also, simply, meant you felt "more good."[11]

If you wanted to get happier, then you had to become less unhappy. If your happiness was decreasing, then your unhappiness was increasing.

The truth is, however, that feelings associated with happiness and unhappiness can coexist. Modern psychological research has shown that positive and negative emotions are in fact separable, allowing us to conclude that happiness is **not** the absence of unhappiness.[12] (Remember, happiness and feelings are not the same, but they go together like dinner and the smell of dinner.) Positive and negative emotions can each be felt in the absence of the other, simultaneously, or in rapid succession. Some neuroscientists believe that happy and unhappy feelings largely correspond to activity in different hemispheres of the brain, noting that negative emotions align with activity on the left side of the face, positive on the right.[13]

People generally assess their feelings as a blend. "I feel good" means happiness > unhappiness. However, when instructed to do so, they separate out their positive and negative emotions fairly accurately. For example, researchers in one experiment found that people could identify their emotions about 90 percent of the time.[14] They classified their feelings as purely positive about 41 percent of the time and purely negative about 16 percent of the time. The rest (33 percent) were mixed between positive and negative. All together, then, people discern some negative feelings about half the time, on average, and positive feelings about three-quarters of the time.

In an experiment, people were asked to go through their entire days and think about how much positive or negative "affect"—that is, feeling—they got from each activity, instead of blending the two emotions together.[15] In general, people had more positive feelings than negative feelings, but this depended a lot on the activity. Some activities (like socializing) had really high positive feelings and low negative ones. Others (like taking care of children or working) were more of a blend. The activities that were most negative and least positive were commuting and spending time with one's boss. (Obviously, then, it's definitely best not to commute with your boss.)

What all of this means is that you could have high happiness **and** high unhappiness at the same time, or vice versa. One does not depend on the other. It might sound like splitting hairs here, but this is actually a crucial point. If you believe you have to eradicate your feelings of unhappiness before you start getting happier, you're going to be unnecessarily held back by the perfectly normal negative feelings of everyday life, and you're going to miss out on understanding what makes you **you.**

YOUR UNIQUE MIX OF HAPPINESS AND UNHAPPINESS

We all have our own natural mix of happiness and unhappiness, depending on our circumstances and character, and our job is to use the mix we're given to best effect. The first task in doing that is learning where, in fact, we are.

One way to get evidence of your natural happy-unhappy mix is by measuring your levels of positive and negative affect—mood—and how they compare to others', using the Positive and Negative Affect Schedule, or PANAS. PANAS measures the intensity and frequency of positive and negative affect, and was invented by three psychologists at Southern Methodist University and the University of Minnesota in 1988.[16] PANAS indicates whether you tend to experience higher or lower positive and negative emotional states than average.

To take the test, find a time when you feel relatively neutral about life—say, right after lunch. Don't pick a time when you are unusually stressed out or happier than normal. The test will ask you how deeply you feel a series of emotions. Answer in general, or on average—not at this very moment.

You have five possible answers for each emotion:

1 = very slightly or not at all

2 = a little

3 = moderately

4 = quite a bit

5 = extremely

Assign these scores to the following twenty emotions:

1. Interested
2. Distressed

3. Excited
4. Upset
5. Strong
6. Guilty
7. Scared
8. Hostile
9. Enthusiastic
10. Proud
11. Irritable
12. Alert
13. Ashamed
14. Inspired
15. Nervous
16. Determined
17. Attentive
18. Jittery
19. Active
20. Afraid

Now, calculate your positive affect by summing your scores for questions 1, 3, 5, 9, 10, 12, 14, 16,

17, and 19. Calculate your negative affect by summing your scores for questions 2, 4, 6, 7, 8, 11, 13, 15, 18, and 20.

Unless you are the highly unusual person who is right at the average on both positive (about 35) and negative (about 18), you will fall into one of four quadrants, as illustrated in Figure 1.[17] If you have above-average positive affect and above-average negative affect, you're one of the "Mad Scientists," who are always spun up about something. If you're below-average positive and below-average negative, you're a sober and cool "Judge." "Cheerleaders," with above-average positive and below-average negative, celebrate the good in everything and don't dwell on

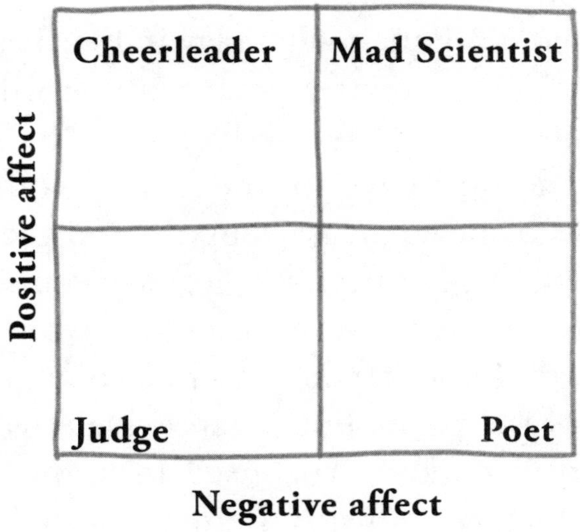

Cheerleader	Mad Scientist
Judge	Poet

Positive affect (vertical axis); Negative affect (horizontal axis)

FIGURE 1: The four types of people, based on positive and negative affect

the bad. "Poets," who register below-average positive and above-average negative, have trouble enjoying good things, and always know when there is a threat lurking.

We know, we know: you wish you were in the cheerleader quadrant. But we can't all be cheerleaders, and the world needs the other profiles as well. On a moment's reflection, you'll likely realize that it would be a nightmare if everyone saw only the bright side of everything, because we'd keep making the same mistakes again and again. Poets are valuable for their perspective and creativity. (And everyone looks great in a black turtleneck.) Life is more interesting with Mad Scientists in the mix. And Judges keep us all from blowing ourselves up with impulsive ideas.

You have a unique role to play in life. Your profile is a gift. But no matter what your profile is, you have room to increase the happiness in your life. To do that, you have to understand your natural happiness blend, manage yourself, and then play to your strengths. For example, let's say you are a Mad Scientist. You will tend to react very strongly, good and bad, to things in your life. This might make you the life of the party, but it can exhaust your loved ones and coworkers. You need to know this, and work to manage your strong emotions and reactions.

Maybe you are a Judge. You are cool as a cucumber, and perfect for jobs like surgeon or spy (or anything in which keeping your head is an advantage—like raising teenagers). But with friends and loved ones, you might seem a little too unenthusiastic at times. This knowledge can be useful so that you work to muster a little more passion than comes naturally, for the sake of others.

Or perhaps you are a Poet. When everyone says everything's great, you say, "Not so fast." This is important, because it can literally or figuratively save lives—Poets see problems before others do. But it can make you pessimistic and hard to be around at times, and you can tend toward melancholy. You need to learn how to brighten up your assessments and not catastrophize.

Even a Cheerleader needs emotional self-management. Everyone loves being a Cheerleader, but keep in mind that you will probably avoid bad news and have a hard time delivering it. That's not always a good thing! You will need to work on that so you can give people the truth, see things accurately in life, and not say everything is going to be all right when it just isn't true.

Learning your PANAS profile—your natural blend of happy and unhappy feelings—can help you get happier because it indicates how to manage your tendencies, but in separating the two sides, it also points out vividly that your happiness does **not** depend on your unhappiness. The PANAS test is empowering, because using it, many people understand themselves for the first time, and see that there is nothing weird about or wrong with them.

For example, some people go for many years thinking they are defective because they experience more negative feelings than others around them, and have a hard time mustering as much enthusiasm as others. They learn they are simply Poets. **And the world needs Poets.**

APPRECIATING BAD FEELINGS

How should you think about your unhappiness? First of all, you should be thankful for it. The human brain reserves space specifically to process negative emotions.[18] And thank goodness: negative emotions don't just help us achieve enjoyment, satisfaction, and purpose; they also keep us alive. Threats are more likely to hurt us than treats are to help us, which is why you probably wouldn't accept a simple coin flip to either double your savings or go completely broke. As a matter of fact, if you have any kind of nest egg you've worked for, you probably wouldn't even take nine-to-one odds for this bet, because the one-in-ten chance of losing everything is a prospect too terrible to face.

Thus, we are better suited to processing unhappy feelings than happy ones, to keep us safe and alert to danger. This is called negativity bias.[19] Negative emotions also help us to learn valuable lessons so we don't make mistakes again and again. That's the case made by the late psychotherapist Emmy Gut, who showed in her research that negative feelings can be a helpful response to problems in the environment, leading us to pay appropriate attention and come up with solutions.[20] In other words, when we are sad or angry about something, we may be more likely to fix it. And that, of course, leads us to be happier in the long run.

For example, think about **regret.** No one enjoys their regrets in life. Some declare they will have no regrets at all (even to the point of tattooing NO REGRETS on their bodies) so they can be happier. It's true that when unanalyzed and unmanaged, regret can be poison for your well-being. Obsessive regret is implicated in depression and anxiety, especially among ruminators: the people who go over and over their regrets excessively, cutting a deep groove into their daily life.[21] Too much regret can even affect your hormones and immune system.[22]

But going to the other extreme is even worse. Extinguishing your regrets doesn't put you on a path to freedom; it consigns you to making the same mistakes over and over again. True freedom requires that we put regret in its proper place in our lives and learn from it without letting it weigh us down.

As uncomfortable as it is, regret is an amazing cognitive feat. It requires that you go back to a past scenario, imagine that you acted differently to change it, and with that new scenario in mind, arrive at a different present—and then compare that fictional present with the one you are experiencing in reality.

For example, if today your relationship with your partner has soured, your regret might mentally take you back to last year. You would remember your own pettiness and irritability, and then imagine yourself showing more patience and being kind instead of hurtful at key moments. Then you would fast-forward to today and see a relationship that is flourishing instead of languishing.

This process is why, while uncomfortable, regret leads to learning. As Daniel Pink, author of a whole book on regret, says, "If we reckon with our regrets properly, they can sharpen our decisions and improve our performance."[23] Instead of letting the specter of your failed relationship make you miserable, by simply wishing it had turned out differently, you can be honest with yourself about what went wrong and use that knowledge to enjoy better relationships in the future.

Another area of life where unhappiness helps us is creativity. Artists are known for being a bit gloomy and finding their inspiration in darkness—the low-positive, high-negative profile is called the Poet for a reason. No surprise that it was a famous poet, John Keats, who wrote, "Do you not see how necessary a World of Pains and troubles is to school an intelligence and make it a soul?"[24]

Scientists have found that Keats was right. One study even measured the effect of unhappiness on the productivity of artists, looking at (among others) the composer Ludwig van Beethoven, who was most productive after his setbacks in health (he went progressively deaf) and family (he was the guardian of his nephew Karl, with whom he had a miserable relationship).[25] The research found that among great composers like Beethoven, a 37 percent increase in sadness led to, on average, one extra major composition.

The reason for this is that when people are sad, they focus on the unpleasant parts of their lives. This tends to stimulate a part of the brain called the ventrolateral prefrontal cortex, which allows us to focus intensely on other complex problems as well—like writing a business plan, or a book, or a symphony—or to figure out a solution to a complicated life problem.[26]

Some psychologists believe that the best target to shoot for is just enough unhappiness to be in a group we might call "second-happiest." In 2007, a group of researchers asked college students to rate their net well-being on a scale from "unhappy" to "very happy."[27] Like a lot of general well-being tests, this was intended to measure something like "happiness minus unhappiness." They compared the results with participants' academic results (GPA, missed classes) and social indicators (number of close friends, time spent dating). Though the "very happy" participants had the best social lives, they performed worse in school than those who were merely "happy."

The researchers then examined a data set from

another study that rated incoming college freshmen's "cheerfulness" and tracked their income nearly two decades later. They found that the most cheerful in 1976 were not the highest earners in 1995; that distinction once again went to the second-highest group, which rated their cheerfulness as "above average" but not in the highest 10 percent.

Fine, you might be saying, the happiest people didn't earn the most—you might take that trade. But other research suggests this is because of a lack of caution; since negative emotions can help us assess threats, it stands to reason that too much good feeling can lead us to disregard these threats. And in fact, the highest levels of purely positive emotion have been connected to engaging in dangerous behaviors such as alcohol and drug use and binge eating.[28] Good feelings now, bad feelings later.

Here's the bottom line: Without unhappiness, you wouldn't survive, learn, or come up with good ideas. Even if you **could** get rid of your unhappiness, it would be a huge mistake. The secret to the best life is to **accept** your unhappiness (so you can learn and grow) and manage the feelings that result.

BE GRATEFUL FOR THE BEES, NOT JUST THE HONEY

To see our lives clearly, to get unstuck from our problems, and to see the opportunities in our futures, we need to see happiness and unhappiness differently than most people do: happiness is not the goal, and unhappiness is not the enemy. (Of course, we are not talking here about medical issues, like anxiety and depression. These are real maladies that require care and treatment. Rather, we mean the suffering and trouble that everyone faces in life.)

None of this is to say that we should shun good feelings, or that we're foolish for wanting to be less unhappy. On the contrary, the desire for greater joy and less sadness is natural and normal. However, making the quest for positive feelings—and the fight to banish negative ones—the highest or only goal is a costly and counterproductive life strategy. Unmitigated happiness is impossible to achieve (in this mortal coil, at least), and chasing it can be dangerous and deleterious to our success. More important, doing so sacrifices many of the elements of a good life.

Perhaps you are wondering if we are suggesting that you **look** for suffering. There's no need; suffering will find you—and everyone else. The point is that each of us can strive for a rich life in which we not only enjoy delicious honey but can also appreciate the bees responsible for it. This is more than a shift in mindset. It is a new way of life, full of opportunities you have never seen before. By embracing your life without fear, you can manage your emotions. And once you do that, you will be free to build on the pillars that will set you on the path to getting happier for the rest of your life.

Understanding happiness and unhappiness is necessary, which is why we started with this topic. But it is only the first step in building a better life. The second step is managing our positive and negative emotions, so we get stronger and smarter and spend less time distracting ourselves from the parts of life we don't enjoy. We will cover this in the next three chapters.

Managing Your Emotions

A Note from Oprah

I've spent some of my happiest moments sitting under a tree with a good book to read. Or napping in front of a crackling fire snuggling with my dogs. Or puttering around my warm kitchen on a chilly, rainy day, assembling ingredients for a hearty stew. Part of the good feeling is a deep and powerful sense of having everything I need right there. And that is the great lesson of this book. If you want to make yourself happier, you already have everything you need to do so, within you, at any moment, at **this** moment, today.

That last sentence incorporates two lessons we've already learned: First, that it's about happi**er**—a relative, contextualized, fluid condition, not some perfect fixed ideal of nirvana. And second, that happier is not a state of being, but a state of doing—not a thing you wait around and hope for, but an achievable change you actively work toward.

This is one of the things I admire about Arthur as a teacher: he does such a good job defining his terms. One reason I'm sure you'll find this book so helpful is that it gives you a language for talking about—and even more important, for thinking about—happiness. Having a language turns what for most of us is an abstract and vague concept into something much more concrete—something we can understand, consider from different angles, experiment with, play around with. You'll learn a few science-y terms (hello, **behavioral inhibition system**). You'll also relearn, in the specific context of happiness, some very familiar words (**optimism** versus **hope, empathy** versus **compassion**). You'll be introduced to several Arthur-isms—concepts that are terrifically useful because they're terrifically sticky, like **emotional caffeine** and **useless friends.**

But the two most valuable things you'll learn—the words you should tape to your refrigerator or frame and hang on the wall someplace where you'll see them five or ten times a day—are these: "Your emotions are signals to your conscious brain that something is going on that requires your attention and action—that's all they are. Your conscious brain, if you choose to use it, gets to decide how you will respond to them." Once more for good measure: **Your emotions are only signals. And you get to decide how you'll respond to them.** The emotion is the tap on the shoulder, the elbow nudge in your side. What you do about it is completely your call.

You see what that means, right? All the times when you've felt overwhelmed by your feelings, when it's felt as though you're a prisoner of those feelings, when it's seemed as though the feelings are driving the bus and the best you can do is buckle up—you don't have to live like that anymore. There are strategies you can use to take back the wheel. As Arthur will explain, this doesn't mean you'll never again have to deal with anger or fear or jealousy or sorrow or disappointment, but that's precisely the point: You **can deal** with them. You feel the feel, then take the wheel. **You get to decide how you'll respond.**

One of the most trying times in my life was when I was literally on trial, back in 1998. You may have heard of it: I was sued by Texas beef producers for saying something about hamburgers. Now, to put this in perspective, I wasn't on trial for my life. If the verdict hadn't gone my way, I wouldn't have had to go to prison. Still, being on trial is a challenging and exhausting experience. It was difficult and stressful, and it's never a good feeling to be wrongly accused.

And yet, looking back, I would say that during those six weeks I spent in Amarillo, I had reason to be happy. By which I mean **my** version of happy, which is content. On the personality test Arthur shared in the previous chapter, I'm a Judge—I generally don't have super-high highs or super-low lows.

(By the way, in case you're wondering, Arthur is a Mad Scientist. It turns out this combination makes a great team, because Judges and Mad Scientists complement each other.)

It's a wonderful thing to be able to make yourself content in trying circumstances. It's as though you have a ledger: yes, in the minus column there might be something difficult or bad or unpleasant, but there's also a plus column. In Amarillo, my plus column had kind people who wished me well every morning at the courthouse entrance. And a bed-and-breakfast I delighted in. It was clean. I had a comfortable bed. I could take a hot bath every night. There was pie in the refrigerator. (For me, pie means a lot. Not kidding.) I was able to keep my beloved cocker spaniels, Sophie and Solomon, there. And I was able to keep working, taping the **Oprah** show every day after five p.m. when court was over.

Despite my circumstances, in that bed-and-breakfast I had everything I needed, including the thing I may have needed most: gratitude. It's an emotion I highly recommend for anyone who's going through a trial—any trial life might have in store—and it's one Arthur will be talking about in the next section. As you read, I humbly offer you two Oprah-isms to keep in mind: **feel the feel, then take the wheel.** And **happierness.**

Two

The Power of Metacognition

Viktor Frankl, whom we met in the previous chapter, lived through problems most of us can't even imagine. A Jewish psychiatrist from Austria, he was arrested with his loved ones and deported by the Germans to Nazi concentration camps, where he spent nearly four years, until the end of the war.[1] Of those captured, he was the only survivor in his family; his father, mother, wife, and brother all perished. He himself narrowly escaped death many times, and suffered profound brutality.

After the Allied liberation and his release, Frankl returned to his home in Vienna. Reflecting on his experience, in 1946 he published his memoir of life in the concentration camp. It was a global bestseller, and a chronicle of hope in the midst of suffering. It inspired generations of people all over the world, with its simple message that life can be lived with beauty even under the worst circumstances.

Frankl's message was not that life will automatically be good, however, which it obviously isn't. Nor was it that we can somehow escape pain with some special mind trick. He acknowledges that every life has suffering—some a lot more than others. Further, as a psychiatrist, he knew that we react to suffering with negative emotion, which is natural. But a bad life is not our fate, because we have a choice as to how to respond to our emotions. In Frankl's words, "Everything can be taken from a man but one thing: the last of the human freedoms—to choose one's attitude in any given set of circumstances, to choose one's own way."

In other words, you can't choose your feelings, but you can choose your reaction to your feelings. What he was saying is that if someone abandons you, you **will** feel sadness and anger, but you can **choose** whether to be bitter as a result, and thus affect how quickly you will recover. If someone you love gets sick, you **will** be afraid, but you can **choose** how you express this fear, and how it affects your life.

Feelings, in the enterprise of your life, are like weather to a construction company. If it rains or snows or is unseasonably hot, it affects the ability to get work done. But the right response is not trying to change the weather (which would be impossible) or wishing the weather were different (which doesn't help). It is having contingency plans in place for bad weather, being ready, and managing projects in a way that is appropriate to the conditions on a given day.

The process of managing this weather is called metacognition. Metacognition (which technically means "thinking about thinking") is the act of experiencing your emotions consciously, separating them from your behavior, and refusing to be controlled by them.[2]

Metacognition begins with understanding what emotions are and how they work. From there, you can learn some basic strategies for reframing emotions about your present and your past. And with some practice, you'll be able to stop letting your feelings direct your behavior—**conscious you** can be the adult in charge.

YOUR BRAIN, ON FEELINGS

In the previous chapter, we explained that happiness and unhappiness are not the same thing as positive and negative feelings. Feelings are **associated** with happiness and unhappiness, however, and are something we experience forcefully and directly every day. Left unmanaged, they can run amok, making getting happier hard or impossible. Think of this using the metaphor once again of food versus the **smell** of food. The food itself is the most important thing, but if the smell is all wrong, the meal is spoiled. Therefore, while we already touched on emotions, and you measured your affect levels using PANAS, here we need to dig more deeply into the science of emotions.

The most basic understanding of emotions starts with what neuroscientist Paul D. MacLean in the 1970s called the triune brain.[3] If you have heard this before, it's probably because the renowned astrophysicist Carl Sagan made the idea famous in his books and popular television show, **Cosmos,** in the 1980s. This is a theory that human brains evolved over millions of years in three distinct stages.

According to MacLean, the oldest part is the brain stem, sometimes called the reptilian brain because it does things that even lizards can do, like regulating instinctive behaviors and motor functions. The second is the limbic system, or paleomammalian brain, which is more recently evolved and translates basic stimuli into emotions that we feel, signaling to us what's going on around us and thus how we should react. Finally, there is the neocortex, which MacLean suggested is the newest part—the most human, or neomammalian, brain. This is the part that governs decision-making, perception, judgment, and language.

A lot of newer research argues that this three-part model is inaccurate because it isn't clear when each part evolved, and the functions are not so neatly segregated.[4] For example, while the limbic system is primarily responsible for feelings that we believe "happen to us," the neocortex is not purely analytical and participates in complex ways in emotional responses to our environment.

Without getting into technical scientific controversies about evolution and specific brain functions, it is still useful to think of your brain engaged in a series of three functions to keep you alive and thriving.

1. **Detection.** Something happens in your environment. For example, a car—the modern equivalent of a huge predator—is speeding toward you while you are walking through an intersection. Before you are at all conscious of this, the image is processed by the retinas of the eyes (a part of the brain outside your skull!), sending the information to the visual cortex of your brain, located in the occipital lobe, at the very back and bottom of your head.[5]

2. **Reaction.** Your amygdala—a part of the limbic system deep within your brain—receives a signal that there is a threat to your safety, which is translated into the primary emotion of **fear.** This happens in something like 0.074 seconds.[6] The amygdala then sends a signal through the hypothalamus (also part of the limbic system) to the pituitary gland, a pea-shaped organ at the bottom middle of your brain. This tells the adrenal glands down by your kidneys to spit out stress hormones to make your heart pound

and give you a lightning-fast reaction to jump out of the way. Your periaqueductal gray, which also receives a note from your amygdala, tells your body to move.[7]

3. **Decision.** Meanwhile, your prefrontal cortex—the large mass of tissue right behind your forehead—is getting a signal about what's happening. Your brain stem and limbic system have already saved your life, but now you have to decide consciously how to react. Laugh it off? Shake your fist? You decide, using your prefrontal cortex. Recognition of the feelings in your body caused by the stress hormones can alter that decision.

In this case, the emotion of fear has helped save your life. Remember that unhappiness is important because it helps us to learn and improve. Similarly, negative emotions are crucial because they tell us how to react to the world in a way that helps us survive and thrive. Negative emotions are protective against threats like predators; positive emotions reward us for things that we need, like good food. When neuroscientists look at the character Spock on **Star Trek**—a Vulcan who is humanlike but does not express or react to emotions—they scoff that he'd be dead in a week.

This is the most basic argument for being thankful for bad feelings. Next time you are regretting negative feelings and wishing you didn't have them, think about this. They aren't fun, but that's the point. Getting your attention and making you act is how they protect you.

PRIMARY AND COMPLEX EMOTIONS

You have two types of emotions: primary (sometimes called basic) and complex. The first can be felt by themselves, or in combinations that make up the second. Neuroscientists disagree on the exact classification of the primary positive emotions—neuroscience is a relatively new field, and neuroscientists still disagree on a lot of things. But there is fairly wide agreement that the primary negative emotions are sadness, anger, disgust, and fear.[8] None of these emotions are fun, but they are protective. Fear and anger help us respond to threats with fight-or-flight reactions. Disgust alerts us to pathogens by making us avoid contact with something. Sadness makes us want to avoid losing the things and people we need (which explains grief, the psychological distress of being unable to locate a loved one).

Of course, these emotions can be maladapted. For example, while fear of rejection by others is an evolved trait from a time when it meant being cast out of your tribe and wandering the frozen tundra and dying alone, today you might feel it if someone says something critical about you on Twitter. While disgust is a trait helping you smell rotting food before you eat it, today a politician might encourage you to feel it for someone who disagrees with you politically. That's why we need to learn how to **manage** our emotions to live a better life.

Positive emotions usually include joy, which psychologists define as "a feeling of extreme gladness, delight, or exultation . . . arising from a sense of well-being or satisfaction."[9] It is highly pleasurable but fleeting. This makes it very different from the way a lot of religious thinkers define joy, which is more of a lasting inner contentment because of one's relationship with God. Christians define it as a "fruit of the spirit," a well-being that transcends our earthly circumstances.

For neuroscientists and psychologists, joy is a reward for meeting an objective or getting something you want, and it thus makes you continue to strive for the things in life that keep you alive and likely to find mates. As you can see, this positive emotion is similar to the negative ones, but it pulls us toward things instead of pushing us away.

Another positive primary emotion some researchers include on the list is interest. Interest is pleasurable. Humans **hate** boring things and **love** interesting things. Of course, tastes differ. Some people find soccer interesting and baseball boring. Some people adore science documentaries, and others are fascinated by cooking shows. Despite individual differences, the overall reason for this emotion is that humans make progress and prosper when they learn new things. Thus, evolution favors the people who love learning and rewards them with pleasure.

Complex emotions include shame, guilt, and contempt, which are cocktails of the primary emotions. For example, contempt is the conviction that someone or something is totally worthless. That's actually a blend of anger and disgust. You can see how it might help you avoid something terrible for you in society, but you can also imagine how treating others with contempt because of, say, their religion, could be a really bad idea—and something to manage.

METACOGNITION: MANAGING YOUR EMOTIONS

Your emotions are signals to your conscious brain that something is going on that requires your attention and action—that's all they are. Your conscious brain, if you choose to use it, gets to decide how you will respond to them. Think of metacognition as moving the experience of an emotion from the limbic system of the brain into your prefrontal cortex. You might compare it to the process of taking petroleum from the well (your limbic system) to a gas refinery (the prefrontal cortex), where it can be made into something you can use purposively.

We all know the feeling of lashing out when angry and then feeling sorry afterward, or shrieking in fear at something without thinking and then being embarrassed. You might say this is being "authentic," but it is also failing to be metacognitive. When you tell your young child, who is having a tantrum, "Use your words!" you are telling her to be metacognitive: to use her prefrontal cortex instead of just the limbic system. Similarly, metacognition is what you were taught to do when you are angry: before saying anything, count to ten. That is basically giving your prefrontal cortex time to catch up to your limbic system so it can decide how to react. Social scientists refer to people who react automatically without thinking as "limbic," and now you know why.

By the way, the advice to count to ten can be made a little more precise. Thomas Jefferson once wrote, "When angry, count ten, before you speak; if very angry, an [**sic**] hundred."[10] In other words, count longer the angrier you are, or the lower your general level of self-control. One good rule of thumb devised by psychologists is to wait thirty seconds while imagining the consequences of saying what's in your head.[11] Say you receive an insulting email from a client at work and want to fire back an indignant response. Don't write back yet. Instead, slowly count to thirty, imagine your boss reading the exchange (which she might), then imagine seeing the person face-to-face after he reads your response. Your response will be much better, because your prefrontal cortex, not your limbic system, answered the email.

Metacognition doesn't mean you can avoid negative feelings. Rather, it means you can understand them, learn from them, and make sure they don't lead to detrimental actions, which is principally how they become a source of misery in your life. A moment of fear is not necessarily a big deal; it can even be an interesting bit of data—remember, bad feelings are normal and fine. The fear becomes a problem when it makes you behave with hostility or timidity, which hurts you and others for no good reason.

Let's now turn to some ways to apply these ideas to our lives.

WHEN YOU CAN'T CHANGE THE WORLD, CHANGE HOW YOU EXPERIENCE IT INSTEAD

Everyone—even the most privileged among us—has life conditions they would like to change. As the early sixth-century Roman philosopher Boethius put it, "One has abundant riches, but is shamed by his ignoble birth. Another is conspicuous for his nobility, but through the embarrassments of poverty would prefer to be obscure. A third, richly endowed with both, laments the loneliness of an unwedded life."[12]

Sometimes it's possible to change your circumstances. If you hate your job, you can usually look for a new one. If you are in a bad relationship, you can try to improve it, or leave it. But sometimes it isn't practical or even possible. Maybe you hate the weather where you live, but you have family there and a good job, so leaving wouldn't make sense. Maybe you have been diagnosed with a chronic illness for which there are no promising treatment options. Perhaps your romantic partner has left you against your wishes and cannot be persuaded otherwise. Maybe there is something you don't like about your body that isn't possible to change. Maybe you are even in prison.

Here, metacognition comes to the rescue. Between the conditions around you and your response to them is a space to think and make decisions. In this space, you have freedom. You can choose to try remodeling the world, or you can start by changing your **reaction** to it.

Changing how you experience your negative emotions can be much easier than changing your physical reality, even if it seems unnatural. Your emotions can seem out of your control at the best of times, and even more so during a crisis—which is exactly when managing them would give you the greatest benefit. That can be blamed in part on biology. As you read a minute ago, negative emotions such as anger and fear activate the amygdala, which increases vigilance toward threats and improves your ability to detect and avoid danger. In other words, stress makes you fight, flee, or freeze—not think, "What would a prudent reaction be at this moment? Let's consider the options." This makes good evolutionary sense: half a million years ago, taking time to manage your emotions would have made you a tiger's lunch.

In the modern world, however, stress and anxiety are usually chronic, not episodic.[13] Odds are, you no longer need your amygdala to help you outrun the tiger without asking your conscious brain's permission. Instead, you use it to handle the nonlethal problems that pester you all day long. Your work is stressing you out, for example, or you aren't getting along with your spouse. Even if you don't have tigers to outrun, you can't relax in your cave, because these ordinary things are bothering you.

No surprise, then, that chronic stress often leads to maladaptive coping mechanisms in modern life.[14] These include the misuse of drugs and alcohol, rumination on the sources of stress, self-harm, and self-blaming. These responses don't just fail to provide long-term relief; they can further compound your problems through addiction, depression, and increased anxiety. What these coping techniques do is try to change the outside world—at least as you perceive it. People who misuse alcohol often say that a few drinks turn off the day's anxieties like a switch; problems (temporarily) are less threatening.

Metacognition offers a much better, healthier, and more permanent solution. Consider the emotions that your circumstances are stimulating in you. Observe them as if they're happening to someone else, and accept them. Write them down to make sure they are completely conscious. Then consider how you can choose reactions not based on your negative emotions, but rather based on the outcomes you prefer in your life.

For example, let's imagine you have a job that is really bringing you down. Let's say you are bored and stressed, and your boss isn't competent. You come home every day tired and frustrated, and you wind up drinking too much and watching a lot of dumb television to distract your mind. Tomorrow, try a new tactic. During the day, take a few minutes every hour or so, and ask, "How am I feeling?" Jot it down. Then after work, journal your experiences and feelings over the course of the day. Also write down how you responded to these feelings, and which responses were more and less constructive. Do this for two weeks, and you will find you are feeling more in control and acting in more productive ways. You will also be able to start seeing how you can manage your outside environment better, perhaps making a timeline to update your résumé and asking a few people for job market advice, and then you might actually start looking for something new. (We'll offer a few more lessons like this at the end of the chapter.)

The Roman philosopher Boethius, it turns out, was a master of this, and in circumstances much worse than yours or mine. His were more or less like Viktor Frankl's, in fact. He wrote the words quoted previously from a prison cell while awaiting execution in 524 CE, after being accused of conspiracy against the Ostrogothic King Theodoric—a crime of which he was likely not guilty, but for which he was ultimately executed.[15] Boethius could not change his unfair circumstances. However, he could and did change his attitude toward them. "So true is it that nothing is wretched, but thinking makes it so," he wrote, "and conversely every lot is happy if borne with equanimity."[16] To take this to heart and act on it is one of the greatest secrets to increased well-being, but it doesn't have to be a secret. If Boethius could be metacognitive, so can we.

IF YOU DON'T LIKE YOUR PAST, REWRITE IT

You can manage bad feelings, and decide how to react when dealing with bad circumstances. But what about bad **memories**? We can't change those, right? Wrong: metacognition gives us this power.

"At home I dream that at Naples . . . I can be intoxicated with beauty, and lose my sadness," the American philosopher Ralph Waldo Emerson wrote in his essay "Self-Reliance" in 1841.[17] "I pack my trunk, embrace my friends, embark on the sea, and at last wake up in Naples." Sounds wonderful! But then he continues: "And there beside me is the stern fact, the sad self, unrelenting, identical, that I fled from." You can't escape your past, because it travels with you into the future, inside your head. Your memories are the first thing you unpack in Naples.

You can't alter history. You can, however, change your **perception** of it. The next best thing to a time machine is rewriting the story of your memories using metacognition, making the baggage of your past a little lighter on your shoulders as you travel through the present and future.

Humans are time travelers by nature; in fact, scientists have found that we may retain memories of the past precisely so that we can envision and predict the future.[18] Imagine a beach in Spain you would like to visit but never have; the picture in your head might look suspiciously like that beach in Florida from last year. This feat explains why we are so successful as a species: past events give us a crystal ball, which we can use to decide what to do and what to avoid doing.

Modern neuroscience shows that memory is more about reconstruction than retrieval. Each time we conjure up the past, several parts of the brain (including the angular gyrus and the hippocampus) piece together various bits of stored information to assemble a memory.[19] This process is a biological marvel but prone to change with time, as researchers have shown in various ways over the past few decades. For example, shortly after the explosion of the **Challenger** space shuttle in 1986, two psychologists asked university students to recount in detail how they had heard the news of the event.[20] Thirty months later, they asked the same students the same question. In 93 percent of the cases, the accounts were inconsistent, despite the respondents remembering the details vividly and feeling confident in their memories. You might have experienced something similar if, say, you and your sister differ in your recollection of a particularly contentious Thanksgiving.

The reason your memories change is that you construct stories of past events from fragments of memories in accordance with your current self-narratives.[21] You look to days gone by to figure out who you are and why you are doing what you're doing now. To make past information fit your current circumstances, friends, and enterprises, you unconsciously paraphrase your history.

Your shifting memories aren't necessarily inaccurate; rather, they are assembled from partial sets of details, and the exact details you remember change each time you dust a memory off. You and your sister might simply remember different aspects of that Thanksgiving dinner that reinforce your different current circumstances: she says the day was ruined by Aunt Marge (and currently isn't on speaking terms with Aunt Marge); you (who love Marge today) say there was a minor disagreement at the table, but no harm was done.

The particular details you retrieve about past events generally correspond with your current emotional state. For example, researchers have observed that when you are feeling afraid, you tend to construct memories that focus on the sources of threats and remember the past as more full of specific things that hurt you than you otherwise would.[22] In contrast, if you are happy today, your memories will probably be broader and more general. Neither set of memories is erroneous—they are just reconstructed in different ways, based on current emotions.

The fact that your current conditions and feelings influence how you reconstruct memories gives you a lot of power to change your understanding of the past. And if you consciously reconstruct the past more positively, it can help you make decisions about the future—to make useful alterations but avoid changing your present arbitrarily in hopes of a better life.

The next time you want to make a positive change in your life, don't limit your imagination to a change of scenery or the people around you. Start with the backdrop of your life, the very thing that is probably making you restless in the first place. Maybe you want to escape the city where you spent the torturous months of coronavirus shutdowns—which perhaps made you feel isolated and lonely, or harmed your relationships—by moving. Before you get on Zillow, interrogate those painful memories; don't let them roam around by themselves. Instead, think of the sweet moments you've had at home, the kindness you received during those uncertain early pandemic days, and the lessons you learned about yourself. Maybe in the end you **will** decide to leave for Naples. Whether you go or stay, your consciously managed past will make a fine travel companion.

PRACTICING METACOGNITION

Metacognition requires practice, especially if you haven't ever thought about it before. There are four practical ways to get started. First, when you experience intense emotion, simply observe your feelings.

The Buddha taught his followers that to manage emotions, one must observe them as if they were happening to someone else.[23] In this way, one can understand them consciously and let them pass away naturally instead of allowing them to turn into something destructive. Try this yourself when, for example, you have a strong disagreement with your partner or a friend and are feeling angry. Sit quietly and think about the feelings you are experiencing. Imagine them moving physically from your limbic system into your prefrontal cortex. There, observe the anger as if it were happening to someone else.

Then say to yourself, "I am not this anger. It will not manage me or make my decisions for me." This will leave you calmer and more empowered.

Second, as we touched on briefly before, journal your emotions. You may have noticed that when you are upset, if you write about what you are feeling, you immediately feel better. Journaling is in fact one of the best ways to achieve metacognition, because it forces you to translate inchoate feelings into specific thoughts, an action that requires your prefrontal cortex.[24] This in turn creates emotional knowledge and regulation, which provide a sense of control. Recent research shows this clearly. In one study, college students who were assigned structured self-reflective journaling were better able to understand and regulate their feelings about school.[25]

For example, if you are feeling frantic about all the things you need to do, without metacognition there is no way to organize the problem in your mind. Your limbic system is designed to send alarms, not make lists. On a busy day, start with your coffee and calmly make a list of the things you need to do, in order of importance. Your prefrontal cortex is now in charge and you will feel much more in control. You will also have the presence of mind to decide which things get done today, which you will leave until tomorrow, and which you might even decide to do . . . never.

As another example, say you are in a relationship

that is souring against your wishes. Don't use a confrontational (limbic) reaction right off the bat. Instead, take a few days to record what is happening as accurately as possible, as well as your reaction to it. Write down different ways you might react constructively, based on different possible responses from the other person. You will find that you are calmer and better able to cope with the situation, even if it feels unfixable.

Third, keep a database of positive memories, not just negative ones. Mood and memory exist in a feedback loop: bad memories lead to bad feelings, which lead you to reconstruct bad memories. When you are in a highly limbic state, your mind can be saying everything is terrible and always will be, even though that is surely wrong. However, if you purposely conjure up happier memories, you can interrupt this doom loop. Researchers have shown that asking people to think of happy things from their past can improve their mood.[26] You can reap similar benefits in a systematic way by keeping a journal of happy memories and reviewing it when you feel down or out of control.

Fourth, look for meaning and learning in the hard parts of life. Every life contains authentic bad memories. We're not suggesting that you try to reconstruct a past that expunges them or makes them rosy. In some cases, that would be impossible—they are just too painful. Furthermore, some terrible memories can lead us to learning and progress or keep us from repeating mistakes.

Try methodically to see how such painful memories help you learn and grow. Scholars have shown that when people reflect on difficult experiences with the explicit goal of finding meaning and improving themselves, they tend to give better advice, make better decisions, and solve problems more effectively.[27]

In your journal, reserve a section for painful experiences, writing them down right afterward. Leave two lines below each entry. After one month, return to the journal and write in the first blank line what you learned from that bad experience in the intervening period. After six months, fill in the second line with the positives that ultimately came from it. You will be amazed at how this exercise changes your perspective on your past.

For example, say you are passed over for a promotion at work. You are understandably disappointed and hurt, and you want to either vent about it to friends or put it out of your mind. Before you do either of those things, write down "Passed over for promotion" in your journal, with the date. In a month, go back to it, and record something constructive that you learned, such as "I mostly got over the disappointment after only about five days." Then, after six months, go back and write down something beneficial, such as "I started looking for a new job, and found one I like better."

NOW, CHOOSE THE EMOTIONS YOU WANT

When it comes to our emotions, most of us have more power than we think. We don't have to be managed by our feelings. We don't have to hope that tomorrow will be a happy day so we can enjoy our lives, or dread our negative feelings because they will make our happiness impossible. How our emotions affect us, and our reaction to them, can be **our** decision.

Our decision-making doesn't have to stop there. Frequently, we have a choice of emotions themselves—because there is more than one reasonable way to feel about the situation at hand. This is not to say we can or should feel happy when someone we love dies, of course, which would be inappropriate. Rather, there are many times when there are two emotional options that match the circumstances we face, and one is better than the other for our happiness (and that of others). The next chapter reveals how to see the better option and grab it.

Three

Choose a Better Emotion

Most likely, you are a regular user of caffeine in some form. Most Americans are.[1] Caffeine is the mostly widely used drug in our society, by far.

Did you ever stop to wonder how it works? When you ingest caffeine, it quickly enters your brain, where it competes with a chemical called adenosine. Adenosine is a neuromodulator, which sends a signal from one part of your brain to another. A neuron shoots it out, and then another neuron's receptor, perfectly sized to the adenosine molecule, sucks it up to get the information it contains about how you are supposed to feel.[2]

Adenosine's job is to make you feel tired when it plugs into its receptors. At the end of a long day, you produce a lot of adenosine so you know bedtime is coming and it's time to relax. If you didn't sleep well enough (or maybe even if you did), you'll still have some in there in the morning, making you feel groggy. That's where caffeine comes in. This molecule is shaped almost exactly like adenosine, so it fits into adenosine's receptors. Then, when adenosine shows up to make you sleepy or keep you tired, it can't plug in because caffeine is sitting in there already. In truth, caffeine doesn't pep you up—it simply prevents you from feeling drowsy. With enough caffeine, there's almost no adenosine plugged in at all, so you lose all fatigue and feel jittery.

Most people use caffeine because they aren't content with the way they feel naturally, and want better outcomes in mood and work. It does so through substitution of one molecule for another.

Caffeine is a good metaphor for the next principle of emotional self-management: You often don't have to accept the emotion you feel first. Rather, you can substitute a better one that you want.

Your feelings at any moment are being produced to give you an effect that your brain believes is appropriate. For example, somebody cuts you off in traffic, and your brain interprets this as a good reason for you to get angry. It lights up your amygdala and makes you ready to fight—or at least insult the other driver.

Just maybe, however, you don't want to act that way. You don't want to ruin your morning, or have your kids see you lose your temper. You know that you'll feel ashamed of yourself later.

So you want to downregulate that feeling and act in a different way—which might be a little less natural, but will lead to a better outcome. In the case of the rude driver, that isn't to stop the other driver and give him or her a kiss; rather, it might be to simply take it in stride instead of getting mad.

Now remember, getting rid of negative emotions is neither possible nor desirable. You need anger, sadness, fear, and disgust, just like you need adenosine so you can fall asleep at night and relax during the day. But sometimes you want to substitute caffeine for some of your adenosine, and sometimes you want to replace some of your negative emotions in the same way—by temporarily occupying your emotional receptors with something that also fits and is more constructive, leading you to act the way you **want,** not the way you **feel.**

This chapter gives you four ways to do so. We should note here that doing this isn't **quite** as easy and simple as having a cup of coffee. At first it doesn't feel natural to choose an emotion. We have learned since childhood that when you stub your toe, you say "Ouch!" not "Thanks." Emotional substitution is a skill that takes practice, not just an insight that changes everything at once. With practice and dedication, it can become quite automatic, and you will love the results.

HAPPY THANKSGIVING

Think back to the last time you got a performance review at work or a written evaluation in school. Maybe it was positive: lots of compliments and pats on the back. But then there was that one mild criticism . . . a little thorn among the roses. That's what you focused on, right? You knew the evaluation was good, but that little dig from your boss or teacher put it all in doubt. You knew it was silly, but it bugged you for a few days.

You did this because Mother Nature gave you a little gift called negativity bias: a tendency to focus on negative information far more than positive information.[3] The reason is simple: compliments are nice, but nothing happens when we ignore them. But we ignore criticism at our peril. A couple thousand years ago, that could mean being cast out of the tribe. Today it can mean losing your job or strife with a friend. So we naturally focus on negative information.

This might be a good way for a caveman to stay alive, but it is generally a distortion of reality today. You can be sitting in first class on an airplane and feel annoyed that the coffee is a little too cold. Think of all the ways that life is better today than it was when you were a child, and notice that we still always seem to be complaining.

Further, people are terrible at discriminating

between negative information that matters and that which doesn't. Emotionally, you get the same feeling from a random person who insults you in traffic (which doesn't matter) as you do from a letter from the IRS (which can matter a lot). This is because the "sensitivity" of your negativity bias is too high. You need to be able to turn it down so you can see the difference between negative signals and pay attention only to the very few that matter.

The single best way to grasp the reality of good things in life and turn down the noise that makes real threats hard to distinguish from petty ones is to occupy some of the negative emotion receptors with a different, positive feeling. The most effective of these positive feelings is gratitude.

Many people see gratitude as something that happens to them because of their circumstances, which can make it feel out of reach in bad times. That's the wrong way to approach it. Gratitude isn't a feeling that materializes in response to your circumstances. It is a life practice. And even if you feel that you have little to be grateful for right now, you can—and should—engage in it.

Researchers have shown that you can call gratitude into existence by choosing to focus on the things for which you are grateful—which we all have—instead of the negatives in your life. For example, writing in 2018, four psychologists randomly split a sample of 153 human subjects into groups that were assigned either to remember something they were grateful for or to think about something unrelated.[4] The result was amazing: the grateful-remembering group experienced more than five times as much positive emotion as the control group.

Scientists have investigated why gratitude raises positive emotion so reliably, and found several explanations. It stimulates the medial prefrontal cortex, part of the brain's reward circuit.[5] Gratitude can make us more resilient, and enhance relationships by strengthening romantic ties, bolstering friendships, and creating family bonds that endure during times of crisis.[6] It also improves many health indicators, such as blood pressure and diet.[7]

Gratitude makes us better people, too. Approximately two thousand years ago, the Roman philosopher Cicero wrote that gratitude "is not only the greatest, but is also the parent of all the other virtues."[8] Modern research shows that he was probably right. Gratitude can make us more generous with others, more patient, and less materialistic.[9]

Think of how you treat others when you are grateful, and you'll see this immediately. For example, after you get a raise and promotion at work, you walk into a coffee shop and are extra nice to the barista.

The best way to start practicing gratitude is by including it in the journal you use to be more metacognitive. Your journal should list in particular the things in the past for which you are grateful (for example, kindness and love from others) so you don't forget these things. A 2012 study of nearly three thousand people found that when people agreed with the statements "I have so much in life to be thankful for" and "I am grateful for a wide variety of people," they experienced positive emotions and fewer symptoms of depression.[10] Look at these grateful memories regularly—every day or at least every week—to remember and train your mind to do this automatically in difficult moments.

One caution: Don't pretend you feel grateful for the things you aren't actually grateful for. You don't need to roll down the window and thank the rude driver for being so nasty. You shouldn't write "Painful case of shingles" on your gratitude list; you are trying to be grateful **in spite of** that. Forced gratitude can undermine your motivation to be grateful—think of being forced to say thank you or write thank-you notes as a child, and about whether you actually felt thankful in the moment.[11] Accept the things you aren't really grateful for; give thanks for the things you truly are.

Gratitude is a good general technique, but you can apply it in moments of acute negativity as well for immediate relief, especially when facing a situation you are dreading. Say, for instance, you have a family gathering that is going to be hard to face. Spend time beforehand contemplating the things for which you truly are grateful and that are totally unrelated to the gathering. Focus on the friendships you hold most dear, having a job you enjoy, or the fact that you are in good health. This will help put you in a thankful—and happier—frame of mind, making the situation at hand a lot easier to enjoy.

One way to make gratitude even more effective is prayer or meditation. Some researchers have noticed that increasing the practice of prayer is strongly associated with gratitude, even among people who aren't devoutly religious.[12] If you don't want to try prayer, a similar contemplative exercise can help, such as a quiet walk in which you repeat the phrase "I am blessed and will bless others."

Another technique for increasing gratitude: contemplate your death. No, really. Researchers found in 2011 that when people vividly imagined their demise, their sense of gratitude increased by 11 percent on average.[13] Happiness researchers rarely see single interventions with this kind of effect. So, if you're having trouble mustering any gratitude and need it badly, dedicate a few minutes to thinking about all the ways you might perish. When you don't actually die, you'll feel rather grateful indeed. No matter how bad that family gathering is, at least you're alive to see it!

Here's an exercise for increasing gratitude in your life.

1. On Sunday night, take thirty minutes and write down the five things in your life for which you are authentically grateful. It's all right if they seem trivial or silly. Almost everyone else has

ridiculous things on their gratitude lists, too. Make sure one or two, though, involve people you love.

2. Each evening during the week, take out your list and study it for five minutes, one minute for each item. Do it also in the morning if you have time.
3. Update your list each Sunday by adding one or two items.

At the end of five weeks, write down the changes you have seen in your attitude and levels of negative affect. You will likely see what researchers almost always find—a significant improvement. The reason is because your negativity bias doesn't have enough "receptors" to keep you down. Even the true negatives will appear less dire, because you will be naturally treating them more metacognitively and less limbically.

FIND A REASON TO LAUGH

Back in the 1960s and '70s, almost everyone read the magazine **Reader's Digest,** which had a section of jokes called "Laughter, the Best Medicine." It featured a few pages of corny jokes, groaners that were sometimes so bad, you laughed at how terrible they were. Yet it was true: so many people read those jokes because they wanted to feel better. And in truth, humor is excellent emotional caffeine.

Let's start by understanding the science. Read the following sentence:

> When I die, I want to go peacefully in my sleep, like my grandfather . . . not screaming in terror, like his passengers.

If you laughed at that joke, it is because three things happened in your brain in lightning-fast succession. First, you detected an incongruity: you imagined a grandfather lying peacefully in bed, but then you realized he was actually driving a bus (or flying a plane). Second, you resolved the incongruity: Grandpa was asleep at the wheel. Third, the parahippocampal gyrus region of your brain helped you realize the statement wasn't serious, so you felt amusement.[14] And all of that gave you a little bit of joy, which blocked whatever bad feeling you might have had.

After that analysis, the medicine isn't working anymore and you're not laughing. "Humor can be dissected, as a frog can," according to the writer E. B. White, "but the thing dies in the process and the innards are discouraging to any but the pure scientific mind."[15] Jokes aren't funny the second time, or when you explain them, because the surprise is gone. Humor is serious business for blocking negative affect, however, so it's worth understanding the science.

Consuming humor—enjoying jokes—brings joy and relieves suffering. Your brain won't buy it if you try to convince it that you are cheerful when you are sad. But finding humor is just different enough from suffering's opposite that it slides right into the negativity receptor.

Researchers find that it works with amazing reliability. In a 2010 study, one group of senior citizens received "humor therapy"—daily jokes, laughter exercises, funny stories, and the like—for eight weeks.[16] A second group did not receive this therapy. When the study started, both groups reported similar happiness. At the end of the experiment, the people in the first group reported feeling 42 percent happier than they had at the beginning. They were 35 percent happier than the second group, and experienced decreases in pain and loneliness.

Being funny, however, is the one dimension of a sense of humor that does not appear to boost happiness, which is sometimes called the "sad-clown paradox." In a 2010 experiment, researchers asked people to write captions for cartoons and come up with jokes in response to everyday frustrating situations.[17] They found no significant relationship between being funny (as judged by outside reviewers) and getting happier. Another study found that professional comedians score above population norms on scales measuring anhedonia (the inability to feel pleasure).[18]

Note that humor doesn't just block your emotional adenosine—it blocks others' as well. Humor has an almost anesthetic quality to it, lowering the focus on pain and allowing us to remember the joys in life together, even during the worst of times. In fact, there are cases throughout history of people using humor in terrible mass tragedies. For example, the Italian writer Giovanni Boccaccio finished his book **The Decameron** in about the year 1353, as the Black Death ravaged Europe, probably killing almost a third of the population.[19] The book consisted of one hundred comedic stories told by ten fictional young friends—seven women and three men—quarantining together at a country estate to avoid the pestilence. It was massively popular, relieving the fear of sickness and tedium of isolation for people across Europe as the plague dragged on. It did not avoid the themes of sickness and death, but did not emphasize them, either. The point was that life can be pretty hilarious even under rotten conditions—but finding it so depends on our attitude.

And so it is today. Life has sadness, tragedy, and frustration in abundance. Find the funny parts of it and everyone will be a lot better off. Here are three actionable steps you can take today.

First, reject grimness. It can feel as if the world

presents us with overwhelming challenges. Some feel that lightheartedness is inappropriate when we are concerned about crises and injustice. It is a mistake to think this way, insofar as grimness is not alluring to others, and thus doesn't help attract people to your efforts to make the world better. Of course, there are instances in which humor is misplaced (remember, timing is everything), but fewer than you think. Some of the best eulogies at funerals are the most humorous.

Researchers have found that a particularly humorless ideology is fundamentalism in one's beliefs: "I am right and you are evil."[20] Therefore, it isn't surprising that the current ideological climate in the United States (and many other countries) is also so humorless, or that political extremists are so ready to use their offense at humor as a weapon. To be happier and make others happier, no matter what your politics, don't participate in the war on jokes.

Second, don't worry about being funny. Some people can't tell jokes to save their lives. Either they can never remember the punch line, or they start laughing so hard themselves that no one has any idea what the punch line is. That's fine; for happiness, it's better to consume humor than to supply it. It's also a lot easier. Funny people tend to have particular innate neurological characteristics, and unusually high intelligence.[21] Meanwhile, people who enjoy funny things simply prioritize humor, cultivate the taste for it, and give themselves permission to laugh. To get the happiness benefits of humor, let others tell the jokes; listen and laugh.

Third, stay positive. The type of humor you consume and share matters. Humor, when it doesn't belittle others, or when it makes you laugh at your circumstances, is associated with self-esteem, optimism, and life satisfaction, and with decreases in depression, anxiety, and stress.[22] Humor that attacks others or prompts you to belittle yourself follows the exact opposite pattern: while it can feel satisfying for a moment, it doesn't block negative feelings. (It's like decaf coffee!)

CHOOSE HOPE

One of the worst emotional maladies that can befall any of us is pessimism. We all know the Eeyore types, who always assume the worst will befall them. This goes beyond just being a Poet, who detects actual threats; pessimists **invent** threats. It's often not fun to be around them, and they tend to isolate themselves. To add insult to injury, pessimism isn't generally even a helpful view of the world. On the contrary, researchers find that it tends to cause avoidance and passive behavior in the face of challenges.[23] So if you fall prey to pessimism, you become less proactive and you probably aren't even right about your judgment of the problem.[24]

What's the opposite emotion here we need to beef up to block our pessimism receptors? You might say, "That's obvious: optimism." But that's not quite right.

During the Vietnam War, a US Navy vice admiral named James Stockdale, who was held for more than seven years in a North Vietnamese prison, noticed a surprising trend among his fellow inmates. Some of them survived the appalling conditions; others didn't. Those who didn't tended to be the most optimistic of the group. As Stockdale later told the business author Jim Collins, "They were the ones who said, 'We're going to be out by Christmas.' And Christmas would come, and Christmas would go. . . . And Easter would come, and Easter would go. And then Thanksgiving, and then it would be Christmas again. And they died of a broken heart."[25]

There was a less dire version of this pattern you might have noticed during the coronavirus pandemic. Those who struggled the most were the optimists always predicting a return to normality, only to be disappointed as the pandemic dragged on. Some of the people who did the best were downright pessimistic about the outside world, but they paid less attention to external circumstances and focused more on what they could do to persevere.

There's a word for believing you can make things better without distorting reality: not **optimism,** but

hope. People tend to use hope and optimism as synonyms, but that isn't accurate. In one 2004 study, two psychologists used survey data to parse the two concepts.[26] They determined that "hope focuses more directly on the personal attainment of specific goals, whereas optimism focuses more broadly on the expected quality of future outcomes in general." In other words, optimism is the belief that things will turn out all right; hope makes no such assumption but is a conviction that one can act to make things better in some way.

Hope and optimism can go together, but they don't have to. You can be a hopeless optimist who feels personally helpless but assumes that everything will turn out all right. Or you can be a hopeful pessimist who makes negative predictions about the future but has confidence that you can improve things in your life and others'.

Here's an example that might help. Let's say you have a big health challenge on your hands—not life-threatening, but something you would much prefer to fix, if possible. Your doctor says most likely you are going to have to live with the challenge, and you believe her. However, there are a couple of things you can try—perhaps some exercises or a new drug—and you go all in to do so. While you trust the prognosis (which is not optimistic), you are doing what is within your power to make it better (which is hopeful).

Both optimism and hope can make you feel better, but hope is much more powerful. One study showed that although both drive down the likelihood of illness, hope has a lot more power than optimism in doing so.[27]

Hope involves personal agency, meaning it gives you a sense of power and motivation. In one study, researchers defining hope as "having the will and finding the way" found that high-hope employees are 28 percent more likely to be successful at work and 44 percent more likely to enjoy good health and well-being.[28] A multiyear study of students from two universities in the United Kingdom found that hope, measured in response to self-rated measures such as "I energetically pursue my goals," predicted academic achievement better than intelligence, personality, or even prior achievement.[29]

Hope is more than a "nice to have" for well-being; lacking it can be disastrous. In a 2001 study of older Americans who took a survey between 1992 and 1996, 29 percent of those whom researchers classified as "hopeless" based on their survey answers had died by 1999, versus 11 percent of those who were hopeful—even after correcting for age and self-rated health status.[30]

Some might argue that having hope is mostly a matter of luck—you are born with it. This might be partially true for optimism: one study finds it is 36 percent genetic.[31] Research, on the other hand, has yet to find a genetic link to hope. This is because, as many philosophical and religious traditions teach, it is an active choice. Indeed, it is a theological virtue in Christianity, implying voluntary action, not just happy prediction. To build a better world for others, you **should** be hopeful.

Becoming a more hopeful person might seem like it depends on your circumstances, however. "What if they are hopeless?" you might ask. Well, your circumstances are never hopeless. Furthermore, hope can be practiced and learned, by following three steps.

First, imagine a better future, and detail what makes it so. When you feel a bit hopeless, start changing your outlook. Say, for example, you have a loved one who is not taking hold of his future, is neglecting his education, and is perhaps making destructive personal choices that are leading to bad life outcomes and an unpromising future. You could easily conclude that the situation is hopeless, but you can do more for your loved one's happiness—and your own—if you instead imagine what a better, realistic lifestyle would look like.

Rather than basking in the glow of an amorphous "better" situation and leaving it at that, make a list of the specific elements that will have improved. For example, imagine your loved one going back to school and developing healthier friendships. Imagine him meeting a good romantic partner, and giving up substance use.

Second, envision yourself taking action. If you leave things at the first step and simply convince yourself that better times lie ahead, you will have engaged in optimism, but not yet hope. Envisioning a better future will not, on its own, make it so, but it can help the world when it changes our personal behavior from complaint to action. Thus, the second step in this exercise is to imagine yourself helping in some plausible way to bring about a better future, albeit at the micro level.

Continuing with the preceding example, envision yourself establishing more regular contact with the person, in a friendly, non-scolding way that shows you like and care about him as a person and are not just judging him morally. Imagine asking him to tell you about his hopes for a better future, and your volunteering to help in any way you can. Imagine telling him he can stay at your place when he doesn't have anywhere to go; imagine driving him to school or to a job interview. Avoid illusions of being the invincible savior; instead, imagine doing small, tangible acts.

Now, armed with hope, you can move on to the most important step of all: action. Take your grand vision of improvement and humble ambition to be part of it in a specific way and execute accordingly. Follow through on your ideas to help at the person-to-person level.

TURN EMPATHY INTO COMPASSION

Sometimes your negative emotions are not the ones interfering with your life the most. Rather, it is the emotions of someone close to you. A family member, a spouse, or maybe a friend is suffering, and this becomes the focus of your relationship, dragging you down. You don't want to be callous, but at some point, you need some emotional caffeine to block **their** emotional adenosine in **your** brain. As you will see later in this book, negativity in a family can be passed like a virus if you let it. You might think the best emotion to choose is empathy, but that's not quite right. On the contrary, empathy can make things worse for you.

When **empath** first entered the English lexicon, it was anything but a compliment. The term was coined in a 1956 science-fiction story about beings who could feel others' emotions and used them to exploit workers.[32] The word has since taken on more positive connotations, and when people call themselves empaths today, they usually mean that they are kind and caring enough to feel the pain of others. In contemporary culture, empathy seems like an unalloyed virtue, the kind you'd strive to embody.

As virtues go, however, empathy is overrated. Used excessively and on its own, it can bring harm to empathizers and empathizees alike.

Empathy is not feeling sorry for someone in physical or emotional pain—that's sympathy.[33] Rather, it is mentally putting yourself in the suffering person's shoes to feel their pain. It's the difference between "Get well soon" and "I can imagine how much discomfort you must be feeling right now." Some researchers even hypothesize that empaths have hyperresponsive mirror neurons, which are brain cells that imitate those of others when their behavior is observed.[34] So, for example, you want to cry when you see someone else crying.

Evidence suggests that empathy really can lessen other people's burdens. Participants in a series of experiments documented in 2017 were found to experience significant physical pain relief when hearing someone else express empathy, but not when hearing comments that were unempathetic or neutral.[35] Similarly, patients cope better with bad medical news if their doctors are empathetic, showing they personally understand and feel what the patient is going through.[36]

This relief comes at a cost to the empathetic person. In 2014, researchers showed that training people in empathy tended to raise their negative feelings in response to others' distress.[37] This makes sense: if you take on others' pain, you will have more pain in your own life.

But empathy can also wind up hurting other people. In his book **Against Empathy: The Case for Rational Compassion,** the University of Toronto psychologist Paul Bloom argues that empathy "can lead to irrational and unfair political decisions."[38] For example, politicians might give unfair advantage to people in their own racial or religious group, and thus behave unfairly to others. Bloom even says empathy can "make us worse at being friends, parents, husbands, and wives," because sometimes an act of love involves doing something that causes pain rather than relieving it, such as confronting an awful truth.

You can no doubt think of cases in your own life when feeling too empathetic prevented you or someone else from giving the "tough love" someone may have needed. Going back to the example in the previous section, if instead of helping the loved one you think is making poor life choices, you were simply empathetic, it might relieve his suffering briefly, but it wouldn't help him to get on the right track.

Making empathy a full-fledged virtue and a protective emotional caffeine requires adding a few complementary behaviors that convert it into **compassion.** One comprehensive study of compassion defines it as recognizing suffering, understanding it, and feeling empathy for the sufferer—but also tolerating the uncomfortable feelings they and the suffering person are experiencing and, crucially, acting to alleviate the suffering.[39]

Compassion helps both the sufferer and the helper. In the 2014 study that showed that empathy training worsened mood, some participants were given training in compassion instead.[40] Compared with empathy training, compassion training blocked their negative feelings and thus raised their overall mood after they witnessed the pain of others. Compassion also benefits the sufferer; for example, doctors who are more comfortable around patients in pain may be more successful administering painful treatment, such as acupuncture.[41] Learning to look analytically at others' discomfort and providing help can transform another person's burden into an opportunity for both of you to feel better.

Compassion naturally comes easier for some people than it does for others. Research has shown that compassion is to some degree genetic, and that we may be inherently drawn to people with this trait.[42] However, plenty of evidence also shows that compassion can be learned.[43] The key is to use your conscious faculties to push beyond your feelings. Do the work to become strong in the face of pain and you will benefit yourself and others. There is no label like **empath** for someone who has become especially compassionate, but you'll know it when you achieve it, and others will, too.

To become a more compassionate (and thus happier) person, start by working on your toughness. To be tougher in the face of another's pain doesn't mean feeling it less. Rather, you should learn to feel the pain without being impaired to act. If you ever meet a Marine who has gone through boot camp, they will tell you they faced rigors beyond anything they had ever experienced before in life. They wanted to quit every single day. For combat Marines, boot camp is followed over the next couple of years by many rounds of combat training, but each round seems to get easier and easier. This is because they are learning to function under extreme circumstances. Pain, never far away for a Marine, doesn't much faze him or her anymore.

Compassionate people are like Marines after training: just as likely to feel pain as anyone else, but able to bear it and function. Empathetic doctors relieve pain with their empathy; compassionate doctors can also calmly operate on the patient. Empathetic parents suffer with their adult kids when they are struggling at college; compassionate parents can resist the urge to call the dean or drive over to the university and treat their young adults like children.

Beyond being tough, compassionate people are action oriented. A lot of the time, when people are in pain, they resist an effective cure because it would temporarily be even more painful. A person might walk around for years with a trick knee because they can't bear the thought of an operation and recovery (and research shows that people usually overestimate the pain of surgery).[44] Similarly, people stay in toxic relationships because leaving seems too terrible to deal with.

And these examples make one other important point: we need to choose compassion over empathy with **ourselves,** not just others. A lot of empathetic self-care involves feeling your own pain, but stops before doing something difficult in response to it. Being self-compassionate means doing the hard thing that you actually need to do, notwithstanding your feelings, like getting knee surgery or confronting a relationship issue head-on. You might say that empathy is limbic, whereas compassion is metacognitive.

Empaths can't help others commit to difficult resolutions, because their assistance stops at the victim's feelings. But compassionate people, toughened up to act, can do hard things that the person suffering might not want or like but that are for their own good. Compassion can feel like tough love, giving honest counsel that is difficult to hear, saying goodbye to an employee who is not a suitable fit, or saying no to a disappointed child. This can start a virtuous cycle, in which the recipient of compassion gets a little more resilient and becomes better able to show compassion themselves.

MAKING A BETTER WORLD FOR OTHERS

The emotional-caffeine strategy of self-management in this chapter has a huge virtue besides just crowding out some of the excess negative affect we may experience. We are replacing it instead with emotions we genuinely want: gratitude, humor, hope, and compassion. We want them because they aren't just emotions, they are **virtues.**

As you cultivate these virtues, you'll notice something else: you are more and more focused on other people in a productive and generous way, and less and less focused on yourself. And this is the next principle of emotional self-management.

Four

Focus Less on Yourself

In 2020, psychologists Adam Waytz of Northwestern University and Wilhelm Hofmann of the University of Cologne in Germany set out to answer a question: Do I get happier when I focus on my own desires, or when I focus on doing something for others, instead?[1]

We generally think about the trade-off between self-care and caring for others as one between feeling good and doing what is morally superior. If you take the afternoon off and go shopping, you'll enjoy it. If instead you volunteer at a local charity, you'll miss that fun but be a better person. Obviously, this trade-off has limits; you need to take care of yourself to help others, and helping others can be fun for you. In general, however, this is how we see the "me versus others" choice.

The researchers questioned whether there really was a trade-off at all. They wondered if, just maybe, focusing on others created more happiness for **you** than self-care did. To investigate this idea, they divided 263 participants into three groups, each with a different set of instructions.

1. **Moral Deeds Group:** Today, we would like you to do at least one moral deed for others. By "moral deed for others," we mean doing something that will benefit another person or a group of others. This could be donating to charity, picking up trash (to help the community), giving money to a homeless person, helping someone with their work, giving someone a compliment, giving assistance to a family member, or showing kindness to a stranger. Any act that benefits another person—either directly or indirectly—would be considered a moral deed.

2. **Moral Thoughts Group:** Today, we would like you to think at least one moral thought for others. By "moral thought for others," we mean thinking about another person or group of people in a positive way, thinking good thoughts on their behalf, thinking lucky thoughts for them, praying for them, hoping they succeed, or thinking about how much you care for another person or group of people. Any thought

that is positive toward another person would be considered a moral thought.

3. **Treat Yourself Group:** Today, we would like you to do at least one positive thing for yourself. By "positive thing for yourself," we mean doing something that will benefit you. This could be buying yourself a gift, getting yourself a massage, taking yourself out to a movie, spending time with a friend who will make you happy, giving yourself a break to relax, or enjoying a delicious meal. Any act that benefits you—either directly or indirectly—would be considered a positive thing.

The three groups followed their instructions, and recorded their well-being across eleven dimensions each evening for ten days. At the end, the researchers compiled the results. Not shockingly, in some ways all the strategies were beneficial; for example, all three felt more satisfaction. But in most ways, the results weren't even close. The Moral Deeds Group reported higher scores on a range of well-being measures than the Moral Thoughts Group, and both reported higher scores than the Treat Yourself Group. Those caring for others actively felt greater purpose in life and sense of control, while the others did not. They were also the only ones who felt less anger and social isolation.

The end results were clear, and consistent with a huge body of data showing that focusing less on yourself and your desires will make you happier. This is not to argue you should stop taking care of yourself or stop paying attention to your own needs. As they say on the airlines, you must "put on your own oxygen mask first" when it comes to happiness, so you **can** help others become happier. That's different from thinking about yourself **instead of** others and what is going on outside.

In fact, adopting more of an outward focus on life—observing the world and caring for other people without making so much of life about yourself—is one of the best ways to increase your own well-being, and is the third principle of emotional self-management. This means being good to others as selflessly as possible—as the preceding experiment suggests, of course—but more subtly, it means deflecting your own constant attention from yourself and your desires—by looking in the mirror less, disregarding your reflection on social media, paying less attention to what others think about you, and fighting your tendency to envy people for what they have but you don't.

This part of emotional self-management is not intended to scold or make any of us feel like we are self-centered egomaniacs. Focusing on ourselves is the most normal thing in the world. Yet this doesn't help us get happier. While it isn't always easy, working against this natural tendency gives us relief from the sitcom on loop in our heads that is our daily me-focused lives. With knowledge and practice, an outward focus on life brings major happiness rewards.

YOU ARE ACTUALLY TWO PEOPLE

You may have noticed that you look most normal to yourself when you look in a mirror. A photo always looks less natural, almost as if it were another person. And in fact, philosophers say that you are, in a very real way, two different people—one who sees, and one who is seen. Understanding this can help us a great deal in focusing less inwardly and more on the outside world.

The American philosopher William James explored this idea of two selves in depth. He believed you must be an observer of things around you to survive and thrive, but you must also observe yourself and be observed by others to have any consistent sense of self-concept and self-image.[2] Without observing outwardly, you would get hit by a car or starve. Without being observed, you would have no memory, history, or sense of why you do what you do. When you are driving to work, you are observing traffic and other people to stay safe and get where you are going. But once you are at work, you pay more attention to how others see you, which helps you understand if you're doing a good job.

When you are the observer, it's called being the "I-self" (the seer of things around you). When you are observed, or looking and thinking about yourself, that's called the "me-self" (the one seen). Neither one is a permanent state of mind. The trick for well-being is balancing your I-self and your me-self. And that means increasing the former and decreasing the latter, because most people spend too much time being observed and not enough time observing. We think constantly about ourselves and how others see us; we look in every mirror; we check our mentions on social media; we obsess over our identities.

This brings trouble. As we mentioned in the previous section, focusing more on the world outside is linked to greater happiness, while focusing on yourself and how others see you can lead to unstable moods.[3] Your happiness goes up and down like a yo-yo depending on whether you perceive yourself positively or negatively in a given moment. This instability is hard to bear; no wonder self-absorption is associated with anxiety and depression.[4]

Seeing yourself as an object (looking inward) rather than the subject (looking outward) can also lower your performance in ordinary tasks. Researchers have found in learning experiments that people are less likely to try new things when they are focused on themselves.[5] This makes sense: When you pay too much attention to yourself, you ignore a lot about the outside world. You feel less free when you are worrying about "How am I doing?"

and "What do others think about me?" Little kids sometimes inspire us with their unselfconsciousness, just being themselves, because they often stay for a long time in the I-self state, just observing, acting, and enjoying.

The idea that you should spend more time thinking about the world than about yourself predates modern science and philosophy. For example, it is a core focus of Zen Buddhism, which is fundamentally an attitude of pure outward observation. "Life is an art," the Zen master D. T. Suzuki wrote in 1934, "and like perfect art it should be self-forgetting."[6] Robert Waldinger, a Harvard psychiatry professor and Zen priest, explains it this way: "When I'm aware of the self I call 'Bob,' it's me in relation to the world. When that falls away (in meditation, or when I'm standing in awe of a waterfall), the sense of a self that is separate from everything else subsides and it's just sounds and sensations."[7]

In some traditions, the I-self is not just a ticket to happiness but a connection to the divine. Hindus seek to reveal their **atman,** which is characterized by an innate state of awareness in which one witnesses the world but does not get embroiled in it. Atman is considered a direct link to **Brahman,** the ultimate divine reality. Jesus's teaching that "anyone who wishes to follow me must deny himself" is usually interpreted as focusing on God and other people, but doing so also requires a greater emphasis on the I-self.

You will never eradicate your me-self, of course, but you can certainly increase your happiness by adopting conscious practices that lower the amount of time you spend in an objectified state. Three conscious habits can help.

First, avoid your own reflection. Mirrors are inherently attractive, as are all mirrorlike phenomena, such as social media mentions. We are magnetically drawn to them. But mirrors are not your friend. They encourage even the healthiest people to objectify themselves; for people with self-image-related maladies, they can be sheer misery. In 2001, researchers studying people with body dysmorphic disorder (those who think obsessively about perceived flaws in their bodies) found that the longest time the participants spent looking in the mirror (and thus focusing on the source of their distress) was 3.4 times longer than the longest mirror-gazing session of those who didn't have the disorder.[8]

Take steps to make the version of yourself that the world sees less likely to pop up in front of you. You might consider literally removing all but one or two mirrors from your home and making a rule to not look at yourself more than once in the morning. One fitness model, who had become miserably obsessed with his body and was desperate to return to a healthier, more normal life, went a full year avoiding mirrors and even went so far as to shower in the dark to stop seeing and judging his own physique.[9]

Virtual mirrors are even easier to get rid of than

literal ones. Turn off your social media notifications. Adopt an absolute ban on googling yourself. Turn off self-view on Zoom. Don't take any selfies. This is hard at first, because all these practices of self-observation give such a reliable little hit of the satisfying neuromodulator dopamine. But it gets easier with practice, especially when you experience the relaxation that comes from not looking at yourself.

Second, stop judging things around you so much. Judging might seem like pure observation, but it really isn't. It is turning an observation of the outside world inward and making it about you. For example, if you say, "This weather is awful," this is more about your feelings than it is about the weather. Further, you have just assigned a negative mood to something outside your control.

Making judgments about the world is normal and necessary; we need to do it in order to make cost-benefit decisions. However, many judgments are unhelpful and gratuitous. Do you **really** need to decide that the song you just heard is stupid? Try instead to observe more around you without regard to your opinions. Start by making more purely observational statements rather than values-based ones. Reframe "This coffee is terrible" as "This coffee has a bitter flavor." At first this is very tricky, because we are just so used to judging everything. Once you get the hang of it, it is a huge relief to not have to have an opinion on everything. You will find yourself not weighing in on political debates and giving fewer opinions; this will keep you calmer and in a greater state of inner peace.

Third, spend more time marveling at the world around you. In his research, the University of California, Berkeley, psychologist Dacher Keltner focuses on the experience of awe, which he defines as "the feeling of being in the presence of something vast that transcends your understanding of the world."[10] Among its many benefits, Keltner has found, awe diminishes the sense of self. For example, in one study, he and his colleagues asked people to consider either an experience in nature that was beautiful or a time when they felt pride.[11] Those who thought about nature were twice as likely as those who thought about pride to say that they felt small or insignificant, and nearly a third more likely to say that they felt the presence of something greater than themselves.

Spend more time enjoying things that amaze you. Happiness specialist Gretchen Rubin visits the Metropolitan Museum of Art almost daily, for example. Incorporating awe into your daily life might mean making sure you see the sunset as often as you can or studying astronomy—or whatever it is that blows **your** mind.

One last exercise you might try if you have a free day: use it to wander. In one famous Zen koan (a story that requires philosophical interpretation), a junior monk sees an older monk walking and asks him where he is going.[12] "I am on pilgrimage," the senior monk says. "Where is pilgrimage taking you?" the junior monk asks. "I don't know," the elder answers. "Not knowing is the most intimate."

The senior monk was simply observing where he was walking, without intention or judgment. Some of the most profound and intimate experiences in life come when you can observe your journey without expectation of some destination or external payoff. Try dedicating just one day to being like the senior monk. Start the morning by saying, "I do not know what this day will bring, but I will accept it." Go through the day focusing on things outside yourself, resisting judgment, and avoiding anything self-referential. If you are feeling really adventurous, you could even get in your car and go on a day trip with no set destination.

STOP CARING WHAT **THEY** THINK

There is a well-known Bible verse that says, "Judge not, that ye not be judged."[13] To be focused in a healthy way on others and the outside world grants you the "Judge not" part. Our next lesson gives you the second part of that verse: to not be judged—or at least to not pay attention to the judgment of others, by caring less what they think about you.

It is important to note that caring about and paying attention to others is very different from worrying about what others think **about you.** The first is helpful and good; the second is often egocentric and destructive. In fact, to manage emotions, almost all of us need to work to care less what others think about us. That's even harder than getting rid of all your mirrors, though. Just think of the last time some random person criticized you—someone you would certainly not invite into your home for a conversation, but whom you invited into your head as you stewed about the criticism. Maybe it was a sarcastic barb on social media or a belittling remark at work. You kicked yourself for even caring—but you did care nonetheless. In fact, for most people, a source of stress is what others think of them. Many of them are deeply wounded by criticism, go to extraordinary lengths to gain the admiration of strangers, and lie awake nights wondering about others' opinions of them.

Why is this? Once again, it's Mother Nature making our lives difficult. We are wired to care about what others think of us, and we obsess over it. As the Roman Stoic philosopher Marcus Aurelius observed almost two thousand years ago, "We all love ourselves more than other people, but care more about their opinion than our own," whether they are friends, strangers, or enemies.[14] For happiness, then, thinking of others' opinions of us is even worse than obsessing over ourselves directly.

Paying attention to the opinions of others is

understandable and, to a certain extent, rational. You trust your own opinions; they are saturated with and shaped by those of others who are similar to you; therefore, you trust their opinions as well, whether you want to or not.[15] Thus, if one of your coworkers says some TV show is really great, your opinion of it will probably rise, at least a little bit, and you might decide to try it.

You especially care about others' opinion of you, and evolution explains why: For virtually all of human history, humans' survival depended on membership in close-knit clans and tribes. Before the modern structures of civilization, such as police and supermarkets, being cast out from your group meant certain death from cold, starvation, or predators. This can easily explain why your sense of well-being includes others' approval, as well as why your brain has evolved to activate the same region for physical pain when you face social rejection—the dorsal anterior cingulate cortex, or dACC.[16] (By the way, neuroscientists have noticed that an over-the-counter remedy for physical pain that targets the dACC—acetaminophen, or Tylenol—can also lower negative feelings associated with exclusion!)[17]

Unfortunately, the instinct to want the approval of others is woefully maladapted to modern life. Where once you would have justifiably felt the terror of being expelled into the forest alone, today you might suffer acute anxiety that strangers online will "cancel" you for an ill-considered remark, or passersby will snap a photo of a poor fashion choice and mock it on Instagram for all to see.

This tendency may be natural, but it can drive you around the bend if you let it. If you were a perfectly logical being, you would understand that your fears about what other people think are overblown and rarely worth fretting over. But none of us are perfectly logical, and most of us have been indulging this habit for as long as we can remember.

In the worst cases, anxiety about the approval of others can blow up into a debilitating fear, a psychological condition called allodoxaphobia.[18] Don't worry—it's rare. But even short of that, worrying about the opinions of others can lower your basic competence in ordinary tasks, such as making decisions. When you are thinking about what to do in a particular situation—say, whether to speak up in a group—a network in your brain that psychologists call the behavioral inhibition system (BIS) is naturally activated, which allows you to assess the situation and decide how to act (with a particular focus on the costs of acting inappropriately).[19] When you have enough situational awareness, the BIS is deactivated and the behavioral activation system (BAS), which focuses on rewards, kicks in. However, research shows that concern about the opinions of others can keep the BIS active, impairing your ability to take action.[20] If you tend to leave an interaction kicking yourself over what you should have said but didn't, it may indicate that you are being unduly influenced by concerns over what others think.

One reason you may fear others' opinions is because negative assessments can lead to shame, which is the feeling of being deemed worthless, incompetent, dishonorable, or immoral—and thus, given the weight we place on others' opinions, we begin feeling this way about ourselves. Fearing shame makes sense, because research clearly shows that feeling it is both a symptom of and a trigger for depression and anxiety.[21]

In the **Tao Te Ching,** the ancient Chinese philosopher Lao Tzu wrote, "Care about people's approval and you will be their prisoner."[22] He no doubt intended it as a dire warning, but this is more of a promise and an opportunity. The prison of others' approval is actually one built by you, maintained by you, and guarded by you. You might add a complementary verse to Lao Tzu's original: "Disregard what others think and the prison door will swing open." If you are stuck in the prison of shame and judgment, take heart: you hold the key to your own freedom.[23]

Remember, the goal here is to focus on others but not on their opinion of **you.** One way to do this is to remind yourself that **no one cares.** The ironic thing about feeling bad about yourself because of what people might think of you is that others have many fewer opinions about you—positive or negative—than you might imagine. Studies show that we all consistently overestimate how much people think about us and our failings, leading us to undue inhibition and worse quality of life.[24] Perhaps your followers or neighbors would have a lower opinion of you if they were thinking about you—but they probably aren't. Next time you feel self-conscious, notice that you are thinking about yourself. You can safely assume that everyone around you is doing more or less the same.

Second, rebel against your shame. Because fear of shame is frequently what lurks behind an excessive interest in others' opinions, you should confront your shame directly. Sometimes a bit of shame is healthy and warranted, such as when we say something hurtful to another person out of spite or impatience. Often it is frankly ridiculous, such as being ashamed for, say, accidentally leaving your fly unzipped, or having a bad hair day.

We are definitely **not** recommending that you walk around with your fly down on purpose. But ask yourself: **What am I hiding that I'm a little embarrassed about?** Resolve not to hide it anymore, and thus dominate the useless shame holding you back. We promise that once you metacognitively own the source of your embarrassment and resolve not to be held back by it, you will feel empowered and much happier.

DON'T WATER THE ENVY WEED

Another way we focus on ourselves is by indulging the deadly sin of envy. When we envy, we obsess over what we have or don't have. Once again, this may seem outward-focused, but it is really all about what you wish you had. This tendency spoils our relationships, makes us worse to others, and makes life impossible to enjoy.

In the thirteenth canto of "Purgatorio" in Dante's **Divine Comedy,** the fourteenth-century Italian poet describes the ultimate punishment of people who had fallen prey to envy during their lives. He shows them perched precariously on the edge of a cliff. Because envy started with what they saw, their eyes are wired shut. To avoid falling, they must support themselves upon one another, something they never did in life.[25] This is a pretty grim punishment.

Perhaps you are less concerned than Dante with punishment in the hereafter. There is plenty of evidence that envy, the resentful longing for what someone else possesses, can give you a little bit of hell in the here and now. We all know how envy feels—how it sours our love and dries up our soul. How it makes us think not just about ourselves, but specifically about what **we don't have** that others do. How it brings out the ugly, spiteful phantasms inside us that take pleasure in the suffering of others for no other reason than that their good fortune makes ours feel insufficient in comparison. As the essayist Joseph Epstein has written, "Of the seven deadly sins, only envy is no fun at all."[26] Envy, in short, is a happiness killer.

Unfortunately, it is also completely natural, and no one escapes it entirely. The possible explanations for its natural, evolutionary roots are easy to see. Social comparison is how we gauge our relative place in society, and thus how we know what to strive for in order to stay competitive for resources and viable in mating markets. When we see that we fall behind others, the pain we feel often spurs us to build ourselves up—or to tear others down. All of this could have been life-and-death in caveman times, but it is outdated today. You are unlikely to die alone because your social media posts are less popular than those of others. But the pain can still be just as acute.

How people act in the face of this pain has led some scholars to distinguish between **benign envy** and **malicious envy.**[27] The former is miserable, but is met with a desire for self-improvement and to emulate the envied person. In contrast, malicious envy leads to wholly destructive actions, such as hostile thoughts and behavior intended to harm the other person. Benign envy occurs when you believe that admiration for the other person is deserved; malicious envy kicks in when you believe it isn't.[28] This is why you might envy a famous war hero but wish him no ill, while enjoying the news that a reality star just got arrested.

Envy—especially when malicious—is terrible for you. To begin with, the pain is real. Neuroscientists find that envying other people stimulates your brain's dACC, which, as we already know, is where you process pain.[29] It can also wreck your future. Scholars in 2018 studied eighteen thousand randomly selected individuals and found that their experience of envy was a powerful predictor of worse mental health and lower well-being in the future.[30] Ordinarily, people become psychologically healthier as they age; envy can stunt this trend.

Different people envy different things. For example, some research suggests that what people envy tends to change with age.[31] Young people may be more envious than older folks of educational and social success, good looks, and romantic fortune. Older people generally shrug at these things, but tend to envy people with money. This probably makes sense; early on, you naturally want what you think will give you the best shot at making a good living and starting a family; later on, you seek financial security.

To feel envy, you need to have exposure to people who appear more fortunate than you. That is simple enough in ordinary interactions, but the conditions of envy explode if we expose people to a wide array of strangers curating their lives to look as glamorous, successful, and happy as possible. Obviously, this is a reference to social media. In fact, academics have even used the term **Facebook envy** to capture the uniquely fertile circumstances that social media creates for this destructive emotion.[32] And in experiments, scholars have shown that, indeed, passive Facebook use (although no doubt this is not limited to Facebook) measurably decreases well-being through increased envy.[33]

So what is the remedy for lowering envy to manageable levels in your life? The famous fifteenth-century merchant Cosimo de' Medici compared envy to a virulent, naturally occurring weed.[34] The job is not to try to eradicate it, which would be futile; rather, he taught, **just don't water it.** Here are three ways to do that.

First, focus on the ordinary parts of others' lives. The main way we water that terrible weed is with our attention. We focus intently on the qualities we want but lack. For example, you might envy an entertainer's fame and wealth, and imagine how those qualities would make your life so much easier and more fun. But think a little deeper. Do you **really** believe that entertainer's life is so great? Are her money and fame bringing a healthy marriage? Do they eliminate her sadness and anger? Probably not; perhaps the contrary.

Psychologists have shown that you can use this observation to blunt your envy. In 2017, researchers asked a group to think of demographically similar people whom they considered to have exceptionally good circumstances in their lives. They found that focusing only on these circumstances led to a painful contrast with participants' own lives, and thus to envy.[35] Yet when they were instructed to think about the everyday ups and downs that these people surely also experienced, envy was diminished.

Second, turn off the envy machine. Social media increases envy because it does three things: it shows you the lives of people more fortunate than you; it makes it easier than ever for anyone to flaunt their good fortune to the masses; and it puts you in the same virtual community as people who are not in your real-life community, making you compare yourself with them.[36] Celebrities' and influencers' posts are a particularly potent—and unnecessary—source of envy. The solution is not to ditch social media; it is to unfollow people you don't know and whose posts you simply look at because they have what you want.

Third, reveal your unenviable self. This is similar to rebelling against your shame by living outward instead of inward. While you are working to curtail your envy of others, stop trying to be envied yourself. Wanting to display your strengths and hide your weaknesses from strangers is natural. This might feel good, but it is a mistake. Obscuring the truth to yourself and others is a path to anxiety and unhappiness. And as researchers showed in a 2019 study, when people are honest not just about what they did right but also about how they failed along the way, observers experience less malicious envy.[37] But be careful: Your failures have to be authentic. So-called humblebragging, in which a boast is disguised as humility, can be perceived a mile off and makes you less likable to others.[38]

GET READY FOR THE NEXT STAGE IN BUILDING THE LIFE YOU WANT

The previous three chapters were all about turning away from the attitude that the world has to change for life to improve, to one where you are working on changing yourself and your emotions.

Once again, this does not mean eradicating emotions, even negative ones. Negative feelings in response to tough life circumstances are not fun; they never are. They are hard—for some people, a lot harder than for others. They are also necessary and manageable, and with dedication and practice you can use metacognition to manage them. You can learn to practice emotional substitution, and you can gain enormous relief by focusing less on yourself.

This all takes practice, and it isn't easy. This is "Master's Level" emotional management. You won't be perfect and you will have good and bad days, because these things are hard. But it absolutely can be done, and you can do it. And as you make progress, you will get happier, as will those around you. Even better, emotional self-management sets you free from the distractions we all use to numb our discomfort and equips you to focus on what truly matters.

And what truly matters to build your life is what we turn to next.

Building What Matters

Emotional self-management, the subject of the previous three chapters, makes you much happier as a person, freeing you from being managed by your feelings. It is kind of like a comprehensive program to improve your physical fitness, which makes you feel better and healthier. But getting in great physical shape does more than that; it also makes it possible for you to do a lot of new things to enjoy life even more, like becoming more active and social. Similarly, emotional self-management gets you ready to make some big, positive moves to build a happier life.

As we learned in chapter 1, happiness consists of the macronutrients of enjoyment, satisfaction, and purpose. To build happiness we need to grow in all three of these elements, consistently and consciously.

Before we learn the skills of emotional self-management—metacognition, emotional substitution, and adopting an outward focus—we tend to spend a lot of time doing things that make these macronutrients hard to attain. The reason is that our impulses, amplified by the consumer economy, entertainment, and social media, push us to spend our time focused not on what matters but rather on trivialities and distractions: money and stuff, power or social status, pleasure and comfort, and fame or the attention of others. There's nothing new in these distractions, of course. The thirteenth-century philosopher and theologian Thomas Aquinas listed what he called idols that occupy our days and waste our lives: money, power, pleasure, and prestige.

These idols all stand in the way of enjoyment, satisfaction, and purpose. They substitute pleasure for enjoyment, set our hedonic treadmill on "extra high" to make satisfaction harder to attain and keep, and focus us on things that obviously are trivial, not meaningful. The four idols make getting happier harder.

So why do we pursue them? The same reason we always do self-destructive things when we are unhappy but unable to change our circumstances: distraction. Think of the last time you were sitting in an airport waiting for a flight that was delayed for hours. Frustrated but with no way to fix the situation, you probably started fiddling on your phone to distract yourself and pass the time.

Similarly, the four idols are distractions to numb us to emotional circumstances we dislike and feel we can't control. Don't like how you feel about your marriage? Do some "retail therapy" to get your mind off it for a few minutes. Is work getting you down? Scroll social media or inane YouTube videos for an hour to forget. Feeling lonely? A little celebrity gossip will distract you. Conveniently, we are surrounded by millions of commercial options to indulge those distractions. (Unhappy people make great consumers.)

These distractions are a temporary anesthetic, not a cure for our problems. And while they distract us from uncomfortable feelings, they also distract us from making progress. Even worse, they can become addictions that exacerbate the effect of the emotions controlling us.

Emotional self-management lowers the attractiveness of these distractions. If you could call someone and solve the flight delay, you would immediately do that instead of goofing around on your phone. And when we have the tools to manage our emotions, the world's baubles and time-wasters no longer attract us so much—nor do we have the time to waste on them. We aren't stuck in place anymore. We are willing and able to build for the future instead of frittering away our time in the present.

That raises the next big question: **What exactly should we focus on instead of the idols?** If we want to build happier lives, and we now have the time and energy to do it, what are the pillars on which to build them?

There are thousands of scholarly articles on this question, and many more written by self-improvement gurus. You could compile a list of ten thousand little practices to raise your happiness incrementally. You can find thousands of dubious happiness "hacks" on the internet to adopt (for a monthly subscription fee, of course).

Fortunately, if we look at all the best social science research together, just four big happiness pillars stand out far above all others. These are the most important things to pay attention to in order to build the happiest life each of us can, and thus they deserve the lion's share of our attention as we invest in ourselves and our loved ones. This is where to spend the time, attention, and energy released by emotional self-management.

The four pillars are family, friendship, work, and faith.

- **Family.** These are the people we are given in our lives and generally don't choose (except our spouses).
- **Friendship.** This is the bond with people we love deeply but who aren't our kin.
- **Work.** This is our toil to earn our daily bread, to create value in our lives and in the lives of

others. It might be paid or unpaid, in the marketplace or at home.

- **Faith.** This does not mean a specific religion, but rather is a shorthand term for having a transcendent view and approach to life.

These are the pillars on which a good life is built. This isn't to say nothing else in life is important. Obviously, you need to take care of your health, you need to have fun, you need to sleep, you need to be smart about your finances, and on and on. But family, friends, work, and faith are the Big Four on which almost everything else rests.

Of course, these areas of life are full of challenges—some of them very hard. These are the very challenges we so often distracted ourselves from. But now, with our emotional skills and growing resolve, these challenges in family life, friendship, work, and faith are our opportunities to learn and grow in love and happiness. So that is what we turn to in the next four chapters.

A Note from Oprah

Much of what I know about getting happier comes from experience—my own and that of so many others. Arthur, on the other hand, comes to happiness through research. It's a distinction that applies to us in general: when it comes to explaining something or making a point, I always have a story, he always has a study (or a quote from an ancient philosopher). We're different that way.

And then there's Stedman, my life partner and companion for the past thirty years. The two of us once co-taught a class on leadership at Northwestern University's Kellogg Graduate School of Management, and our students were surprised by how different we were. He's a planner, a strategist. He does nothing without first setting a vision for the outcome, whether he's playing golf or speaking to businessmen in China. I am the opposite, operating in the moment, guided by intuition and instinct to the next right move. He never worries about what other people think. I have spent much of my adult life working to nullify my people-pleasing ways.

And then there's my bestie, Gayle King. In personality-test terms, I'm a Judge, Gayle is a Cheerleader. I stay calm, she gets excited. I like to drive in silence, she likes the radio on (and lordy, does she love to sing along). We'll leave an event together with me saying, "Phew, I can't wait to get home," and Gayle saying, "I could have stayed all night!"

It turns out that Arthur and I **and** Stedman and I **and** Gayle and I are **complementary:** different personalities that mesh together well. And happily for all of us, the research says that's what makes for the strongest and longest-lasting relationships.

Different kinds of relationships are the subject of the next section of this book. The focus starts at close range—you and the way you deal with your family—then progressively zooms out to include your friends, your work and the people you work with, and finally your relationship to "the majesties of the universe," through whatever form of spirituality is right for you.

As you read, you'll begin to appreciate what I think of as the inner-outer paradox—the fact that, as we saw earlier in the book, the surest way to improve your inner world is to focus on the outer world, because happiness inside comes from looking outside. I'm not saying that happiness **depends** on external circumstances; we've already seen that waiting for someone or something else to make you happy is a losing game. My point is that our lives are spent in connection—to other people, to our work, to nature and the divine—and the more we do to improve those connections, the better off we are. So in the next several chapters you'll be thinking about whom and what you interact with and how you can make those interactions better. Whom and what do you surround yourself with? What can you do in the face of conflict? How can you show up more intentionally and serve more meaningfully?

These questions lead to another paradox—maybe, in the context of happiness, **the** paradox—the one I call detached attachment. I have learned to live my life so that I'm attached to the work I do and the things I create and the people who matter to me—but not in a way that involves expectations. It's a lesson I learned the hard way, after the movie **Beloved,** a movie I worked ten years to bring to life, based on a novel I revered, came out. When it bombed at the box office, I sank with it.

Though at the time it seemed that the experience might crush me, what happened with **Beloved** ultimately freed me. Today, everything I do, anything I make, any suggestion I float or advice I give—it's all just an offering. If it works, it works. If it's accepted, it's accepted. If not, I have lost nothing because I had no attachment to a particular result. This has made for a much, much happier life for me, and I wish the same for you. But all I can do is wish it—what you do with it is up to you.

Five

Build Your Imperfect Family

I am happiest when I am home with my family," reports Angela, age forty. Married for fourteen years and the mother of three kids ranging from four to twelve, she considers her family the most important part of her life. She works part-time, but her career definitely takes a back seat to family life.

What about when she is **unhappiest**? When asked this, she thinks for a moment, and then confesses, with a half smile, "I guess that would be when I am home with my family."

Angela's experience isn't unique. Family can bring us to the highest highs and lowest lows. On the one hand, there are few things as deeply satisfying as family harmony. Most people in the United

States and all over the world—in fourteen out of seventeen developed countries surveyed by the Pew Research Center in 2021—consider their families to be the biggest source of meaning in their lives.[1] On the other hand, there are few things more upsetting than family conflict, which can send even the steadiest of souls into a tailspin. Fears about loved ones' health and mortality are the second and fourth most common fears that Americans hold.[2] (Fears number one and three are corrupt government officials and nuclear war, in case you are curious.) With the stakes around it so high, building this first pillar of a happier life is one of the best and most reliable ways to improve well-being.

Most people say they want a "happy family," but what does that mean? By "family," we generally mean the people you live with and are related to, by blood, adoption, or marriage: kids, parents, siblings, and spouses. So far, so good. The harder part is figuring out what it means for a whole family to be arguably "happy," or if it is even possible. If you take your cues from television (generally a bad idea), you will think your goal as a family is to be like those on **Leave It to Beaver** or **The Brady Bunch.** But those families don't exist in real life.

Maybe a happy family depends on the kids. After all, "You're only as happy as your unhappiest child," goes the old saying. One of the worst feelings of despair for parents is seeing your child suffering and not being able to help. So perhaps a happy family is one without unhappy kids. Good luck with that. Is it one where the parents have a perfect marriage, never suffer unemployment or struggle with illness? Never seen it.

In truth, truly "happy" families exist only in the minds of the writers of wholesome family television shows. They don't exist in the wild. In real life, families are made up of people mashed together. This can result in the most mystical kind of love—the love you didn't choose but that was given to you. It inevitably also means plenty of conflict. Even in the best of situations, tension between family members is normal, and crises are par for the course. In one pair of researchers' words, family bonds are frayed by "the give-and-take between autonomy and dependence and the tension between concern and disappointment."[3] That's academic-ese for "Family life can be a huge mess."

There are five common challenges that make family life most complicated, which we will cover in this chapter. Each one bears similarity to the issues we took on in our own heads in the first half of the book, and not surprisingly, each has a solution using the same basic tools. Here's the important thing to remember: challenges are actually opportunities to learn to grow in this unique and powerful area of love, as long as we use the tools we developed earlier in this book.

Challenge 1

CONFLICT

"Happy families are all alike; every unhappy family is unhappy in its own way."

This is the famous opening line from Leo Tolstoy's novel **Anna Karenina.**[4] The story starts in a moment of chaos in the Oblonsky family, where the father has just been discovered having an affair. With the parents distracted and distraught, the children "ran wild all over the house," and every member of the family felt as if there were no sense living together again.

Even if the Oblonskys' exact conflict never afflicted your family, many other conflicts probably have—and they may have led you to intense unhappiness. Perhaps you saw it as evidence that you are doing everything wrong. In truth, family unhappiness due to conflict is a signal that something important is right where it should be. You are upset because your family matters to you. If it weren't true, you would feel the same way about conflict in your own home as you do about conflict in the family down the block: mildly concerned and sympathetic, perhaps, but certainly not miserable.

Furthermore, you know very well that trying to avoid unhappiness is never the right way to make life better. Think of conflict like the bill for a delicious meal at a restaurant: the only way for it to be zero is not to order the meal. Conflict is the cost of abundant love. The objective is not to make it go away—it is to manage it metacognitively, replace it when possible with positive emotions, and blunt it as necessary.

What accounts for family conflict? Generally, it is a misalignment between how family members view their relationships and the roles that they each play—in other words, mismatched expectations. For example, parents tend to see the benefit of family bonds primarily in terms of shared love; children generally view the benefit in terms of exchanges of assistance. According to research, fathers report higher levels of involvement in the relationship than their kids perceive.[5] Similarly, children tend to think that they are doing more to help than their parents think they are.[6] All of this creates resentment, which is only natural when people you love fail to meet your expectations; it is exacerbated when the other party doesn't even seem to notice.

Other areas of unmet expectations are common as well. Children can seem unambitious to parents who struggled to make ends meet early on. The kids might not try hard enough in school; as young adults they might forgo marriage or children, to their parents' disappointment or disapproval. Similarly, parents might withdraw financial support in a way that seems selfish to grown kids, or appear more interested in their own lives than in those of their children and grandchildren. Siblings can fail to support each other in any number of ways.

The most extreme form of unmet expectations is a values breach, in which one family member rejects something about the others' core beliefs. An example of this is a child who rejects the parents' religion, or who declares the parents' beliefs immoral. We hear stories all the time of young adults who come home from college and announce to their parents that they are completely wrong about everything.

Some conflicts result in a rupture to the relationship. Researchers writing in 2015 found that about 11 percent of mothers ages sixty-five to seventy-five with at least two grown children were totally estranged from at least one of them.[7] They found that a values breach was at the root of many of these estrangements, while a violation of behavioral norms (for instance, not practicing their faith) usually was not. (Take a moment and think about what this says: your family generally cares less about how you live and more about what you say about what they believe.)

Acknowledging family conflict is good, because it improves communication and gives you opportunities to solve problems. Conversely, denying family conflict is unhelpful, because family conflicts generally don't die of old age. On the contrary, research shows that without working on conflicts, parent-child and sibling relationships remain strained as everyone involved ages—a phenomenon partly explained by a theory known as the developmental schism hypothesis.[8] So accept the fact that you are like almost every other family, and take the opportunity to make things better. Here are three ways to do so.

First, don't try to read minds. As the years go by, many families fall into a tendency to assume that communication need not be spoken—that everyone understands one another without saying anything. This is an invitation to miscommunication. Evidence shows that it's best to have a clear family policy of speaking for yourself and listening to others.[9] One way to do this is with regular family meetings, where each of you can air issues that are on your mind before they fester into a major problem or misunderstanding.[10] If this is too awkward, then set regular meetings in groups of two for the most sensitive topics. The key isn't asking anyone to change their reactions to your actions or feelings; it's giving them the chance to hear your side of things and respond before you start assuming that you know what their response will be.

Second, live **your** life, but don't ask them to change **their** values. Estrangement within families is a tragedy—perhaps inevitable in cases of abuse, but avoidable in so many clashes of pride. You have to decide yourself whether a schism is warranted, but as the research suggests, family members (especially parents) are likelier to accept lifestyle choices that they disagree with than accept differing values, which they might perceive as a personal rejection.[11]

Perhaps this sounds morally inconsistent or even hypocritical, but it isn't. Many people hold values that they do not share with their loved ones. They can still coexist permanently with these differences of opinion without feeling hurt or angry, precisely because they don't expect anyone else to change their mind. And because they don't insist on agreement, there is no reason to feel aggrieved.

Third, don't treat your family like emotional ATMs. When people treat their family as a one-way valve of help and advice—usually, parents giving and children receiving—the resentment tends, ironically, to go both ways; conversations, visits, and calls become tiresome, repetitive interviews instead of conversations. Our belief is that this stems from a stunted development in the relationship. For example, if you are a young adult, perhaps Mom and Dad still treat you like a youngster; meanwhile, you rarely or never ask about their lives or take a true human interest in them.

Rather than expecting your family members to be bottomless fonts of help and wisdom—or to stop giving you unsolicited advice all the time—take the lead by treating your family the way you do your friends, both generously giving and gratefully accepting emotional support. Research shows that the relationship can be greatly enhanced when adult children and their parents treat each other as individuals with past histories and limitations; in other words, as real people.[12]

Challenge 2

INSUFFICIENT COMPLEMENTARITY

In some family relationships, you sort of expect a fair bit of conflict—say, between adolescents and their parents. But in others, conflict feels like a real threat, because we are told by our culture it is bad. The best example of this is conflict between spouses or romantic partners. Discord in this area almost never feels like a good thing and is seen as evidence that something is wrong.

And how do you avoid conflict with your spouse or partner? By being compatible. If there's one piece of conventional wisdom about romantic life, it's that you need a high level of compatibility. The idea is that there is less discomfort and conflict when your partner is a lot like you. If you find someone compatible, the attraction will be higher and the relationship more successful, or so the thinking goes.

This is wrong. Just consider the evidence from people who are dating. Dating apps, which almost everybody uses, have made compatibility easier and easier to achieve. Before you ever see someone in person you can sort her or him on any number of dimensions, to raise the odds of a good "fit." Less pain, more gain. But here's a weird thing: Most "daters"—people who are not in a committed relationship but would like to be, or people who date casually—are struggling.[13] In a 2020 survey, 67 percent said their dating life was not going well.[14] Three-quarters said that finding someone to date was difficult.

The fact is that the more we achieve compatibility, the harder love gets to find and maintain. From 1989 to 2016, the proportion of people in their twenties who were married fell from 27 percent to 15 percent.[15] And in case you think that's just a commentary on traditional marriage, the same survey shows that the percentage of 18-to-29-year-olds who had not had any sex in a year nearly tripled from 2008 to 2018, from 8 to 23 percent.[16]

Looking for someone who has a lot in common with you is called homophily, and it is natural. As egotistical creatures, we tend to rate those who are similar to us as more appealing (socially and romantically) than those who aren't.[17] Consider the case of political views. According to the online-dating site OkCupid, 85 percent of millennials responding to a 2021 survey said that how a potential date votes is "extremely or very important" to them.[18] And among college students, 71 percent of Democrats and 31 percent of Republicans said that they would not go out on a date with someone who voted for the opposing presidential candidate.[19]

The effects of homophily are even stronger when it comes to education. Researchers have found that educational attainment is the most important dating criterion for millennials, exceeding earning potential, physical attributes, and political and religious affiliations.[20] They also found that 43 percent of daters with a master's degree judge potential partners based on the college they attended.

Some similarity in basic values is no doubt beneficial to a partnership, but too much sameness brings huge costs. Romantic love requires complementarity—that is, differences. A sociologist named Robert Francis Winch advanced this idea in the 1950s by interviewing couples and assessing the personality traits of those who were successful and those who weren't.[21] He found that the happiest couples tended to round out each other's personality—an extrovert and an introvert, for example.

Research has found that strangers assigned to perform a task in pairs feel warmer toward each other when their personalities are complementary than when they're similar.[22] In one study, people described their ideal romantic partners as similar to themselves, but their actual partners' personality traits were uncorrelated with their own.[23] We may think we want partners like ourselves, but we wind up pursuing long-term relationships with people who are different from us.

The attractive force of difference may have

biological roots. Scientists have long known, for example, that children inherit a wider variety of immune defenses when their parents differ greatly in a group of genes called the major histocompatibility complex (MHC). None of us can look at a potential mate and decode her MHC at first sight, but there is evidence that we sense components of it through smell—though we don't realize it, because our olfactory neurons function below the level of consciousness—and that we're more attracted to people whose genes "smell" different from our own.[24] In 1995, Swiss zoologists asked women to sniff T-shirts worn by men they didn't know but who had worn the shirts for two straight days.[25] The women preferred the smelly shirts worn by the men whose MHC genes were most different from their own. Later research on different populations found the same result.[26]

Despite all this evidence that you really shouldn't be searching for a version of yourself when you date, the most common ways that Americans find partners these days—via websites and apps—are smorgasbords of sameness.[27] Algorithms allow people to find dates like themselves with brutal efficiency.[28] It might make for fewer disputes, but in searching for your doppelgänger, you might be overlooking the people who complement you, psychologically and even physically.

This search for compatibility has spilled over into how long-established couples see themselves. If you have been in a relationship for a long time and are struggling to keep it together, you might have assumed that you simply aren't compatible enough. This is possible, of course; every couple needs some things in common. More than likely, the real problem is that you and your partner have not been working to turn your differences into the complementarity a healthy relationship needs.

To get more complementarity into your love life, here are three things to do. First, seek out differences in personality and tastes. For example, if you are dating, look for someone who is not your double on the introvert-extrovert dimension. You will learn a lot from each other (as you will see in the next chapter) if you seek to show each other the joys of going to parties one night and being alone the next. This expands the pool of potential mates and makes life more fun. If you are long married, make a list of the ways your partner is different from you. For example, if you are a worrier and your spouse isn't, it may have driven you crazy that she or he "doesn't care enough" about all the problems in life. Instead, reclassify your spouse as your personal agent in the art of lightening up. (You can be their personal threat spotter.)

Second, focus more on what really matters. Too many couples get hung up on differences that are frankly ridiculous, like political issues. If you need to, make a list together of the ten things in your life you both agree are most important. If you have kids, they will probably be number one. Your extended families, faith, and work will all be near the top. Politics and other bones of contention will be way down at the bottom, if they make the list at all. Now resolve to focus your time together on the important stuff.

Third, if you are dating, let humans make your matches instead of machines. One of the most robust trends in meeting potential mates over the past three decades has been the move away from dates set up by friends. More than half of people ages 54 to 64 have had a blind date (a date set up by others, where the daters are unacquainted) in their life, according to DatingAdvice.com, versus only 20 percent of adults ages 18 to 24.[29] On the surface, this makes some sense: Why waste a whole dinner out trying to meet a person on the basis of someone else's recommendation when a closer match is just a few clicks away?

If you have read this far, you know the reason: traditional blind dates are generally arranged by people who know you and have thought about whether your personality fits with your date's. The less exclusively you rely on an internet-dating profile, the freer you can be from philosophical prejudices, and the more you might rely on more primitive mechanisms—like your nose. This strategy only works, of course, when your friends know eligible matches with whom to set you up. If you ask your friends to help and they consistently come up dry, it may be evidence that you need to expand your social circle.

Challenge 3

THE NEGATIVITY VIRUS

A healthy family is not conflict averse. Conflict is different, however, from chronic negativity, which can spoil family life.

The ambient culture in a family, or in any close-knit group, determines the ability of the members to solve problems. Think of it like the room temperature. If the temperature in your house is a hundred degrees and you are feeling too hot, it doesn't really matter how many clothes you take off—you'll still be too hot. Similarly, a negative culture in a family can make problem-solving impossible, so there is no growth or learning, just chronic unhappiness. This often occurs because of emotional contagion, which psychologists have studied extensively.[30] There's not a particular problem to solve, just a "this sucks" attitude that moves between family members.

Escaping from contagious negative emotions can be difficult, but more to the point, when we truly love others who are suffering—especially our family—we don't **want** to avoid their sadness, frustration, fear, or anxiety. We want to help, and that's good. Just as we shouldn't push away our own negative feelings if we want to grow and solve our problems, we can help those we love by accepting their emotions. But we don't have to take on their unhappiness in the process.

Emotional contagion isn't all negative, of course. You can probably think of people in your life with whom you always seem to be smiling, and others who make you feel warm and generous. Researchers have even studied positive emotional contagion, finding that living within a mile of a friend or family member who becomes happier makes you 25 percent likelier to become happier too.[31] But unhappiness is more contagious and spreads faster.[32] A negative mood in a meeting can infect the whole room in seconds.

Emotions jump between people through a number of mechanisms.[33] The most obvious is conversation, in which you transmit and take on the emotions of others through facial expressions, vocal tone, and posture. You probably have found that when you interact with certain people, you laugh more than normal even when things aren't funny; with others, you complain a lot about things that aren't a problem.

Negative emotional viruses can also be carried home from school or work due, paradoxically, to trust. If you have (or had) little kids, you know that sometimes they are fine all day at school, but when they see you to pick them up, they burst into tears and tell you nothing but horror after horror. This is because they trust you and save the hard stuff all day for you. It feels like punishment but it is actually love. (Grown-ups do this, too, by the way, smiling all day at work and then complaining all evening at home.)

You can "catch" others' emotions physiologically, at least in part. In one experiment, people who inhaled a disgusting smell and those who merely observed a video clip of a person with a disgusted expression had activation in the same parts of the brain.[34] As we saw earlier, similar results have been found in the experience of pain—your brain can sense it simply by seeing someone else who is hurting.[35] This is especially true for people who live together.[36]

The idea of emotional contagion is far from new. More than eighteen hundred years ago, while emperor of Rome, the Stoic philosopher Marcus Aurelius wrote about emotional contagion during the dreaded Antonine Plague.[37] The virus killed as many as two thousand people a day.[38] Still, Marcus wrote, "the corruption of the mind is a pest far worse than any such miasma and vitiation of the air which we breathe around us. The latter is a pestilence for living creatures and affects their life, the former for human beings and affects their humanity."[39] Many people can relate to this after the lockdowns during the COVID pandemic, when their families were all cooped up together. The worst part was often when family members started spreading a terrible attitude, which everybody caught. Similarly, you might prefer to have a cold go around your family on vacation than a foul mood that spoils all the fun.

For a lot of people, the way to avoid negative emotional contagion is to avoid an unhappy person, like you would any communicable disease. But in the cases where love transcends the trouble—when the unhappy person is a spouse, a parent, a child, a sibling—and you choose to stay in the same house, research yields four lessons on how you can help while not allowing it to take over the culture.

First, as we've shown throughout this book, "put on your own oxygen mask first." Work on your own happiness and unhappiness before trying to change your family's. This might seem to contradict the research saying that you should attend more to others. This is different—you need to protect yourself precisely so you **can** help others. Say you are living with or near an unhappy parent. Start each day by tending to your own happiness hygiene: exercise, meditate, call a friend. Give yourself an hour or two of space from the unhappy person, if you can, and focus on what you enjoy and are grateful for. This will give you the happiness reserves you need to lift up someone else.

Second, don't take negativity personally, if you can. Whether there is conflict or not, thinking that someone else's unhappiness is directed specifically toward you is only human. Personalization of negativity and conflict is one of the most powerful ways that unhappiness spreads. Psychologists studying this tendency find that taking negativity personally can lead to rumination, which damages your mental and physical health and ruins your relationships by encouraging you to avoid others and seek revenge.[40]

If you care for an unhappy family member, or even just spend time in the same room as them, remind yourself each day, "It's not my fault, and I won't take this personally." View unhappiness in the same way you would a physical malady. The afflicted person might lash out and blame you because of sheer frustration, but you wouldn't likely accept this blame unless you're the one who injured them.

Third, break the negative culture with surprise. Helping others to be happy is not straightforward. Saying "Cheer up!" for example—what psychologists call reframing—is usually counterproductive.[41] (Just imagine someone saying it to you when you are in a dark mood.) It is much better to get the unhappy person to engage in an activity that you know she likes. Research has shown that actively engaging in an enjoyable activity improves mood more than doing nothing, suppressing the bad mood, or envisioning good times.[42]

There's a catch, though: the researchers have also found that asking unhappy people to imagine happy activities (a step that is necessary for planning them in advance) made them less likely to participate in them. This is because the mood they are being encouraged to imagine seems difficult to attain, making the happy activity seem difficult as well. Even if you ordinarily enjoy riding your bike, it can seem like a chore when you are sad or depressed. Yet if a family member shows up for a spontaneous ride, you might just say yes—and be more likely to enjoy it.

Finally, prevent the spread. So far, the advice here has been geared toward someone who wants to help an unhappy family member. If you are the unhappy one, remember that your loved ones want to help. Doing so might make them happier. More to the point, people who love you don't want you to suffer. Isolating yourself or pretending to be happy just to make other people more comfortable won't benefit anyone.

Instead, actively communicate with others to help keep your relationships healthy. Perhaps this means telling your sibling, "I want you to know that although I am going through a hard time right now, it's not your fault." Or maybe it involves strategic avoidance during particular parts of the day if you tend to feel down at those times. The bottom line is that while you may not be able to will your feelings to improve, you **can** choose how you talk to and treat others, which will give your loved ones more energy to help you when you need it.

Challenge 4

FORGIVENESS

Have you ever heard of the South Indian monkey trap?[43] It consists of a hollowed-out coconut with some rice inside, chained to a stake. The coconut has a hole in the top just large enough for a monkey to insert its hand but not big enough to remove a fistful of rice. While villagers watch from a distance, a hungry monkey reaches in and becomes trapped, unable or unwilling to give up its handful in exchange for its freedom. The villagers can then walk right up and take the monkey away.

Before you say anything unkind about the "dumb monkey," ask yourself whether you are doing more or less the same thing when it comes to conflict in your family life. Do you wish the ambient culture were warmer but you are held back by unresolved anger? If so, you are stuck in an emotional monkey trap.

You're not alone; we all face this situation from time to time in our families, and not just in the obvious cases where we cling to bad feelings by flatly refusing to forgive. Sometimes we sabotage the freedom we crave even when we say we've forgiven others, whether because we still harbor resentment deep down or because we're holding on to offenses to use later against the people who have wronged us. To achieve greater happiness and freedom, we all need to abandon these sorts of partial forgiveness.

In 2018, scholars identified four successful forgiveness strategies that family members use to heal a relationship after a transgression or conflict has occurred: discussion ("Let's talk this through so I can let go of the hurt"), explicit forgiveness ("I forgive you"), nonverbal forgiveness (such as showing affection after a fight), and minimization (which involves classifying the transgression as unimportant and simply choosing to disregard it).[44] Researchers have found that all four of these strategies can be effective, and the one chosen typically depends on the severity of the grievance.[45] For example, discussion is most often used for the worst offenses, such as infidelity in a marriage; minimization and nonverbal forgiveness are most often used for the least problematic issues, such as showing up late for dinner. Explicit forgiveness is probably best for conflicts somewhere in the middle.

The thing about talking through a problem or telling someone, "I forgive you," is that it takes a lot of effort and bruises your pride, and might mean giving up something you want. So sometimes people try shortcuts that **seem** like good ways to resolve a dispute but don't work in the end.

Researchers have written about **conditional forgiveness,** in which vindication is deferred and stipulations are made ("I will forgive you when you do X and Y"), and **pseudo-forgiveness,** which happens when partners decide to suppress or ignore an issue without actually forgiving (not to be confused with minimization, which is different).[46] Conditional forgiveness can provide what researchers call emotional protection—that is, a feeling of safety—to the damaged partner, but can also keep a wound open. Pseudo-forgiveness can prolong an unhappy family relationship because no actual forgiveness takes place, which, the research shows, bodes ill for a relationship's survival.

Conditional and pseudo-forgiveness can look attractive to an aggrieved family member for a number of reasons. Conditional forgiveness offers the victim power over the transgressor, a way to get a desired behavior by holding out the carrot of true forgiveness. Pseudo-forgiveness solves nothing, and can create a grudge that is exploited in moments of irritation. Conditional or pseudo-forgiveness are monkey traps—a handful of emotional rice chosen over freedom from anger and bitterness.

In order to avoid the emotional monkey trap, you'll need to deliberately choose not to fall into it. Releasing the rice takes patience and self-control. First, when you're choosing forgiveness, remember that resolving a conflict is not charity—it primarily benefits **you.** The monkey-trap metaphor makes this clear, and so does the wisdom of the ages. The fifth-century Buddhist sage Buddhaghosa writes that by indulging anger and refusing to forgive, "you are like a man who wants to hit another and picks up a burning ember . . . and so first burns himself."[47] Abundant modern research backs up this idea, showing that forgiveness benefits the forgiver mentally and physically.[48]

Second, widen your conflict-resolution repertoire, especially when what you have tried before isn't working. Perhaps you are a natural minimizer, quick to forgive family members when you can easily dismiss their wrongs against you. The person with whom you have a conflict might believe the severity of the situation is too great to be resolved this way. If you're the one who's been wronged, escalate to explicit forgiveness. If the problem is mutual, try discussion, and talk it out.

And third, don't dismiss minimization too quickly. In many cases, abandoning a conflict rather than trying to solve it is the perfect solution. Ask yourself whether your argument is really important enough to, say, lose contact with your loved one, and act accordingly.

Challenge 5

DISHONESTY

Do you have something you wouldn't dare share with your family? There are a lot of good and logical reasons not to say what you think, especially when others disagree strongly. Offending people feels terrible, and it can lead to unpleasant consequences. Withholding the truth or nodding along might seem practical, despite the fact that you are screaming dissent on the inside.

Just maybe, however, the true act of love is to stop avoiding problems and simply look outward and say what you see—to be courageous, and work toward a family that can take it.

In the 1990s, the writer and psychotherapist Brad Blanton argued just that in his book **Radical Honesty.** When the truth is hard to accept, telling it can have costs, including frayed relationships at home.[49] But Blanton suggested that complete honesty—no white lies, no exceptions—is worth the consequences because it can reduce stress, deepen connections with others, and reduce emotional reactivity.

If you are of the "let's not go there" school of family relations, you might be skeptical of this argument. The research favors honesty nonetheless. Families where people bottle up their feelings and beliefs are not at their best, because they can't bring their full selves to the party. To avoid unhappiness through conflict, they wind up avoiding the happiness that comes from greater intimacy and understanding.

Why do we withhold the truth from—or even lie to—loved ones? As much as we would like to say we are protecting others, it is usually motivated by a focus on ourselves. We want to bolster their opinion of us ("School is going fine"), to avoid conflict

("I agree with your political views"), or to protect others ("You look great, Dad").[50] And then there's sheer laziness. When Mom asks, "How did you like dinner?" you might not have the energy to explain that it was too salty.

Some lies might make life easier, but like most inward-focused behavior, they don't necessarily make life **happier.** When a lie is discovered, it generally harms trust. Even little white lies can do this in family life. When we tell family members things we think they want to hear, we treat them as if we were strangers avoiding conflict. Imagine learning that your spouse found it easier to simply humor you. It would bother you a lot, most likely. For getting happier, closeness beats momentary harmony.

The point of honesty is having enough love for others to be precisely who you are, with complete transparency, even if it is difficult for both of you. Of course, that is easier to say than to do, especially if you have the kind of family with a long history of bottling things up. Fortunately, research from psychologists can help to get you started.

First, before being honest, solicit and accept honesty from others. Some people are quite willing to tell the truth to everyone, no matter who gets offended, but become prickly when presented with truths that they find difficult to accept. The tendency to dish out criticism while being unable to take it is one of the classic traits of narcissists, and to put it less academically, it's the style of the thin-skinned jerk.[51] Such behavior is not an expression of love.

Committing yourself to honesty starts with a commitment to be honest with yourself, and an effort to seek out and accept complete honesty from others, especially loved ones. Ask people for the truth as they see it, starting with those closest to you, and make a commitment not to be offended when they give it. Note that their opinions are not facts, meaning that you have to use your judgment on letting the truth you hear affect your actions. Furthermore, sometimes what you hear will be intended to offend you. You can almost always choose not to take offense.

Second, offer truth to heal, never to harm. What generally holds us back in our ability to persuade one another is that we use our opinions as a weapon instead of as a gift. The same principle applies in even greater force when it comes to the truth. If you keep the truth to yourself when it's convenient and use it to hurt others when you're feeling hurt—as we often do in emotional arguments with family members—then your honesty is not an expression of love. Look for the virtues rather than the imperfections in others. If you do that, most of the truth you speak will be honest appreciation and praise.

Third, make the truth appealing. If you do need

to offer an occasional less-than-positive appraisal, think of a way to reframe it as an opportunity for growth. Rather than telling someone, "You're wrong," say, "Here's a way you can think about this issue differently." Your honest feedback will not always be appreciated, of course, but it can soften the blow.

Maybe your family is such that a policy of real honesty sounds insane to you. Start slowly, and tell your family members it is what you want so you all can understand each other better. Little by little, it will get easier. You all will be less self-protective and more generous. It's kind of like exercise: it will take a while, but then it will become a habit, and then it will feel like a necessity. As you build up this muscle, you can expand honesty outward toward friends and strangers. Always remember, though, to do so while healing and appealing, so that your honesty continues to be an act of love.

NEVER GIVE UP

Family life can be such a unique joy that no effort to build a happier life can neglect it. But even the best-adjusted families are challenging, especially surrounding conflict, compatibility, negativity, forgiveness, and honesty. To sum up, here are the main lessons to make each challenge into a source of growth.

1. Don't avoid conflict, which is your family's opportunity to learn and grow if you understand where it originates and manage it appropriately.
2. You naturally think compatibility is key to relationship success, and difference brings conflict. In truth, you need enough compatibility to function, but not all that much. What you really need is complementarity to complete you as a person.
3. The culture of a family can get sick from the virus of negativity. This is a basic emotional-management issue, but applied to a group instead of to you as an individual.
4. The secret weapon in all families is forgiveness. Almost all unresolved conflict comes down to unresolved resentment, so a practice of forgiving each other explicitly and implicitly is extremely important.
5. Explicit forgiveness and almost all difficult communication require a policy of honesty. When families withhold the truth, they cannot be close.

One last point: If your relationship with your family is especially difficult, working to improve it might sometimes feel like a lost cause. It's easy to throw up your hands. Almost every day, we hear from people all over the world who feel stuck in family problems that seem like they have no solution. Maybe you have said, "I just want to turn my back on those people and get on with my life."

Giving up is almost always a mistake, because "those people" are, in a mystical way, **you.** Your spouse is a completion of you as a person. Your kids provide a rare glimpse into your own past. Your parents are a vision of your future. Your siblings are a representation of how others see you. Giving that up means losing insight into yourself, which is a lost opportunity to gain self-knowledge and make progress as a person. Never give up on the relationships that you did not choose, if at all possible.

But what about the relationships that you have **chosen**? These are your friendships, and that's the next part of our lives to build.

Six

Friendship That Is Deeply Real

"From childhood's hour I have not been as others were," begins Edgar Allan Poe in his haunting 1829 poem "Alone."[1] It details his inability to connect emotionally with other people, to share joys and sorrows. "All I lov'd—**I** lov'd alone."

Poe was not an especially solitary figure; he grew up in a fairly ordinary family, attended school, and served in the military. Yet through it all, he never made any deep human connections, beyond perhaps his cousin Virginia, whom he married when she was thirteen (he was twenty-seven), but who died of tuberculosis a few years later.

According to his obituary, Poe "had few or no friends."[2] Most people were simply not worth his time. It's not that no one wanted his company; it's that **he** didn't much want **theirs.** Again, his obituary: "He had made up his mind upon the numberless complexities of the social world, and the whole system with him was an imposture." His loneliness was self-imposed.

Still, Poe suffered terribly from his lack of friends, self-medicating with alcohol and gambling to numb his pain. Before he died at age forty under circumstances probably involving alcohol poisoning, he confessed his problem. "It has not been in the pursuit of pleasure that I have periled life and reputation and reason," he said. Rather, it was "a sense of insupportable loneliness."[3]

Friendship is the second pillar of building a happier life. Friends can lighten the load of the heaviest days. There are few joys in life as wonderful as seeing a close friend after a long separation. Without friends, no one can thrive. This is the clear conclusion from decades of research.[4] Friendship accounts for almost 60 percent of the difference in happiness between individuals, no matter how introverted or extroverted they are.[5] A life with close friends can be happy even when many other things are going wrong. A life without close friends is like a house in the winter (in Massachusetts) without heat.

Unfortunately, the latter case is increasingly common in our society. Social scientists ask survey questions like "When was the last time you had a private conversation in which you shared personal feelings or problems?" Over the past three decades, the percentage of Americans who would answer "never" to this question has nearly doubled.[6] The percentage of Americans who say they have fewer than three close friends has doubled since 1990.[7]

The reasons for this sound an awful lot like Poe syndrome, but on a mass scale. We are willfully neglecting friendships, and even pushing them away. Our fixation on screens and social media makes it easier to be alone than ever, and many young people even confess that making friends in person now feels awkward or frightening. Our poisonous culture war has broken up perfectly good friendships as well: polling data have shown that about one in six Americans have stopped talking to a friend or family member since 2016 because of politics.[8]

And then, of course, there's COVID. If your life didn't go back to its 2019-era "normal," you are not alone. In a poll conducted in March 2022, 59 percent of respondents said they still had not fully returned to their pre-pandemic activities.[9] More serious for happiness is that many people now prioritize socializing for fun less than they used to in the "before times." In a poll long after the pandemic lockdowns had ended, 21 percent of respondents said that socializing had become more important to them since the coronavirus outbreak, but 35 percent said it had become **less** important.[10] Many feel anxious about socializing, with the number one reason being "not knowing what to say or how to interact."[11] Many of us have simply forgotten how to be friends.

The good news is that it's never too late to relearn friendship skills and restart old relationships. With the right information, nearly all challenges can be met. In this chapter we cover the five challenges that people most commonly face—and how your management skills can turn them into precious opportunities.

Challenge 1

YOUR PERSONALITY

By all accounts, Edgar Allan Poe was an introvert. Perhaps you are, too, and you consider that to be an inhibiting factor in the ability to make more friends and get closer to people. It doesn't have to be this way. In fact, what might have seemed like a high personality barrier to your developing more friendships might be your source of strength, if you use it right.

An easy measure of friendship health is the number of friends you have. You will read here or there that you need three friends, or five, or some other specific number to be happy. This is arbitrary, and it doesn't take account of your specific personality. Here is the rule of thumb: you need at least one close friend besides your spouse, and there is an upper limit of perhaps ten friendships that you can realistically spend enough time on to regard them as close. The exact number depends on you, and especially whether you are an introvert or an extrovert. Neither is better or worse than the other if managed properly, but each personality can experience its own difficulties.

Psychologists see extroversion/introversion as one of the Big Five personality dimensions, along with agreeableness, openness, conscientiousness, and neuroticism.[12] The Big Five theory has been a staple of psychology since the 1980s, but the introvert-extrovert binary was first popularized in 1921 by the Swiss psychiatrist Carl Jung, who posited that the two groups have different primary life goals.[13] The former, he thought, seek to establish autonomy and independence; the latter seek union with others. Those stereotypes have persisted to this day.

The German-born psychologist Hans Eysenck further developed Jung's theory in the 1960s, arguing that our genetics determine our relative extroversion.[14] He believed that cortical arousal—that is, the brain's level of alertness—was more difficult to achieve for extroverts than introverts, so the former seek stimulation in the company of others, ideally the fresh company of new people.[15] Subsequent research has shown mixed results on Eysenck's specific theory, but has found clear cognitive differences between the groups.[16]

In general, extroverts are happier than introverts. In 2001, a group of Oxford scholars broke a sample of survey respondents into four groups: happy extroverts, unhappy extroverts, happy introverts, and unhappy introverts.[17] The happy extroverts outnumbered the happy introverts by about two to one. One common explanation for the happiness differential between introverts and extroverts follows from stereotypes like Jung's and Eysenck's: humans are inherently social animals, so contact brings happiness; extroverts seek out contact, so they are happier.

Extroverts also have a natural edge in enthusiasm—"a passionate state of mind," according to one famous psychoanalyst in the 1960s—which is one of the elements of personality most closely associated with happiness.[18] Enthusiasm about life's events leads to higher enjoyment and a better mood. It also lowers the tendency to withdraw socially.

The fact that introverts prefer solitude and often struggle with sociability doesn't mean that they don't need friends. It just means that new friendships can be harder for them to establish. On the other hand, extroverts face a different challenge: going deep. They tend to flit among lots of people whom they know just a little, and can find an emptiness in their lives when a crisis happens and they don't have anyone to turn to who knows and loves them deeply.

Whether you are an introvert or an extrovert, your personality doesn't have to stand in the way of real friendships, as long as you manage yourself. A good way to do so is by taking a lesson from your opposite. For example, one source of happiness for almost everyone is hope about the future, a sense of life purpose, and self-esteem. Extroverts love to talk to others about the future, their dreams, their life's purpose. As psychologists have long shown, we tend to act according to the commitments we have articulated to others, so the extrovert habit of telling everyone you meet about your goals makes you more likely to reach them and therefore get happier.[19] Introverts find sharing personal hopes and dreams with strangers uncomfortable. What they should do is talk about their castles in the sky with their close, one-on-one friendships.

Meanwhile, extroverts should learn from introverts how to establish and maintain a few deep friendships. This isn't so easy for extroverts, because of their love of crowds, audiences, fresh contact, and excitement. Research shows that extroverts tend to have a lot of low-depth friendships with other extroverts.[20] Extroverts should set a goal each year to deepen one friendship. The way to do this is by organizing your social life specifically around one-on-one conversations about profound things, instead of insisting on congregating in groups. Avoid trivial subjects like hobbies and politics, and move toward deep issues like faith, love—and happiness. This will deepen some of your friendships, and in other cases show you in a hurry that you should look elsewhere for depth.

Challenge 2

EXCESSIVE USEFULNESS

Are your friends useful to you? "I hope so," you might say. But that's a mistake for happiness.

Make a list of the first ten of your friends who pop into your head. Some you would text with any silly thought; others you call only a couple of times a year. Some are people you look up to; others you like, but do not especially admire. You fit into these categories for others as well—maybe you are helpful to one person and a confidant to another. You get different things out of different relationships, which is all well and good.

There is one type of friend almost everyone has: the friend from whom you need or want something. You don't necessarily **use** this person—the benefit might be mutual—but the friendship's core benefit is more than camaraderie. He or she is **useful.**

These are what some social scientists call "expedient friendships"—with people we might call "deal friends"—and they are probably the most common type most of us have.[21] The average adult has roughly sixteen people they would classify as friends, according to one 2019 poll of two thousand Americans.[22] Of these, about three are "friends for life," and five are people they really like. The other eight are not people they would hang out with one-on-one. We can logically infer that these friendships are not an end in themselves but are instrumental to some other goal, such as furthering your career or easing a social dynamic.

Expedient friendships might be a pleasant—and certainly useful—part of life, but they don't usually bring lasting joy and comfort. If you find that your social life is leaving you feeling a little empty and unfulfilled, it might just be that you have too many deal friends and not enough **real** friends.

A lot of research has indicated that one of the best predictors of well-being in middle age is being able to name a few truly close friends.[23] As we just discussed, it doesn't have be ten, and in fact, people tend to down-select their friends to a smaller group as they get older.[24] It has to be more than none, however, and the list should extend beyond your spouse or partner.

All the more reason, then, to take honest stock of your friendships. A convenient way to do this comes from none other than the ancient Greek philosopher Aristotle, in his **Nicomachean Ethics.**[25] He argued that friendships can be classified along a kind of ladder. At the bottom rung—where people are least connected emotionally, so the commitment is weakest—are the deal friends based on utility to each other in work or social life. These are colleagues, partners to a transaction, or simply those who can do each other favors. Higher up are friendships based on pleasure—something you like and admire about the other person, such as their intelligence or sense of humor. At the highest level are friendships of virtue, or what Aristotle called "perfect friendship." These friendships are an end in themselves, and not instrumental to anything else. Aristotle would say they are "complete"—pursued for their own sake and fully realized in the present.

These levels are not mutually exclusive; you can carpool to work with a friend who has the unfailing honesty you strive to emulate. The point is to classify friendships by their principal function.

You might not be able to put it into words, but you probably know how these "perfect" friendships feel. They often feature a shared love for something outside either of you, whether that thing be transcendental (like religion) or just fun (like baseball), but they don't depend on work, or money, or ambition. These are the intimate friendships that bring us deep satisfaction.

In contrast to these real friendships, deal friendships—those at the lowest level on Aristotle's ladder—are less satisfying. They feel incomplete because they don't involve the whole self. If the relationship is necessary to the performance of a job, it might require us to maintain a professional demeanor. We can't afford to risk these connections through confrontation, difficult conversations, or intimacy.

Unfortunately, societal incentives push many of us toward deal friends and away from real friends. The average American worker spends forty hours on the job during the workweek. In leadership, the numbers are much higher.[26] Most of us work with other people, so during the workweek we have less time for our family than for our colleagues, let alone for friends outside of work. In this way, deal friends can easily crowd out real friends, leaving us without the joys of the latter.

So what are you going to do? Start by going back to your list of ten friends. Next to each name, write "real" or "deal." Some of these will be judgment calls, no doubt. That's fine—just do your best. Then, next to the "real friends," ask yourself how many people know you really well—who would notice when you are slightly off and say, "Are you feeling OK today?" How many of these people are you comfortable discussing personal details with? If you struggle to name even two or three, that's a dead giveaway. Even if you can, be honest: When was the last time you actually had that kind of conversation?

If it has been more than a month, you might be kidding yourself about how close you really are.

How many people are left on your list? If there are none besides your spouse or partner, we have identified a problem to solve.

The key to real friendship is a relationship that isn't a stepping stone to something else but rather is a blessing to pursue for its own sake. One way to do this is to make friends not just outside your workplace, but outside all of your professional and educational networks. Strike up a friendship with someone who truly can do nothing for you besides care about you and give you good company.

The quality to look for is **uselessness** (not **worthlessness**—we all have had those friends, too!). That requires showing up in places that are unrelated to your worldly ambitions. Whether it is a house of worship, a bowling league, or a charitable cause unrelated to your work, these are the places where you meet people who might be capable of sharing your loves, but without advancing your career. When you meet someone you like, don't overthink it; invite them over.

In our go-go world, where professional success is valorized above all else and "workism" has become like a religious cult to many, it can be easy to surround ourselves with deal friends.[27] In so doing, we can lose sight of the most basic of human needs: to know others deeply and to be deeply known by them. People of many faiths place this deep knowing at the heart of their relationship with the divine, and it is central to achieving change in psychotherapy.[28]

One of the great paradoxes of love is that our most transcendental need is for people whom, in a worldly sense, we do not need at all. If you are lucky and work toward deepening your relationships, you'll soon find that you have a real friend or two to whom you can say: "I don't need you—I simply love you."

Perfect friendships, as beautiful as they are, can be very hard to maintain. Deal friends generally show up again and again in your life over the course of earning a living; you don't have to make a special effort to maintain them. Real friends are another matter. It is all too easy when your life is busy with family and work to let them fall by the wayside. Someone who was a perfect friend during college might inadvertently become someone you talk to only once or twice a year after you graduate, not because it's what you intend, but because time just passes. By the time you are in middle age, it is quite common to have very few if any of these perfect friends simply due to life pressures and the passage of time.

As with anything else of value, it is important not to leave these relationships to take care of themselves, because they generally won't. With your list of real friends—and people you would like to be on that list—make a concrete plan for staying in touch and seeing one another. Some people will set up a regular time each week to phone or video-chat. Others have a policy of taking each other's calls even while at work or at home (if possible). And it is very wise to find a way to see each other in person for a day or a week every year.

In a busy life, you can't realistically maintain too many of these friendships—perhaps just a couple. Aside from your spouse, you need at least one. To that person, the highest compliment you can pay her or him is "You are useless to me."

Challenge 3

ATTACHMENT TO OPINIONS

Of the many ideas from Eastern religion and philosophy that have permeated Western thinking, the second "noble truth" of Buddhism arguably shines the greatest light on our happiness, or lack thereof. **Samudaya,** as this truth is also known, teaches that attachment is the root of human suffering. To find peace in life, we must be willing to detach ourselves and thus become free of sticky cravings.

This requires that we honestly examine our attachments. What are yours? Money, power, pleasure, prestige—the distractions we sought to be free of with greater emotional self-management?

Dig deeper: just maybe, they are your **opinions.** The Buddha himself named this attachment and its terrible effects more than twenty-four hundred years ago, when he is believed to have said, "Those who grasp at perceptions and views go about butting their heads in the world."[29] More recently, the Vietnamese Buddhist sage Thích Nhất Hạnh wrote in his book **Being Peace,** "Humankind suffers very much from attachment to views."[30]

This attachment can be absolutely disastrous for friendships. There is nothing wrong with holding beliefs strongly, of course. The problem is when a disagreement about those beliefs gets in the way of friendship—the idea that you can't be close to someone because they hold views different from your own. For example, maybe you have very strong political views, and you convince yourself (or let yourself become convinced by others) that your friends who don't hold them are immoral or defective. Or maybe your friends are religiously opposed to something about the way you live, and you conclude that this means they are "denying your humanity." (We're not talking about abuse here—just differences of beliefs.) This is Poe syndrome to a T: you kill a friendship because another person doesn't deserve your company. It is completely self-defeating, because it leads to your own loneliness and isolation.

The solution is, calling back to an earlier chapter, to substitute a chosen virtue for the emotion that is causing harm, one that cultivates love and focuses you on others. This is a virtue in shorter and shorter supply these days: humility. Specifically, a kind that social scientists call epistemic humility, or the recognition that someone else's viewpoint might be useful or interesting, or at least doesn't mean you can't love the person.

Obviously, this is hard—if it weren't, one in six Americans wouldn't have cut off contact with friends and family over politics. But the happiness reward is enormous. In one 2016 study, researchers created a humility score.[31] They found that it was negatively associated with depression and anxiety, and positively associated with happiness and life satisfaction. Furthermore, they found that humility buffers the negative impact of stressful life events. The reason is not something neuroscientifically complicated; humble people just have more real friends, because they are more fun to be with.

As is almost always the case with social science, the data on humility and happiness reinforce what philosophers have long taught. Around the turn of the fifth century, Saint Augustine gave a student three pieces of life advice: "The first part is humility; the second, humility; the third, humility: and this I would continue to repeat as often as you might ask direction."[32]

The humility to admit when we are wrong and to change our beliefs can lead us to make more friends and get happier. But with our defenses arrayed against this virtue, we need a battle plan to alter our way of thinking and acting. Here are three strategies you might want to add to your arsenal.

First, admit quickly when you think you are wrong. People despise entertaining the idea that they aren't right, because they fear that doing so will make them look stupid or incompetent. Thus, left to your limbic tendencies, you will fight to the death for even your worst ideas. This tendency is itself based on an error. In a 2015 study, researchers compared scientists' reactions to being informed that their findings "don't replicate"—that is, they are probably not correct—a common problem in academia.[33] It would be no surprise if scientists, like most people, got defensive when contradicted in this way, or even doubled down on their original results. But the researchers found that this sort of behavior was more harmful to the scientists' reputation than simply admitting they were wrong. The message for the rest of us is this: if you might not be right, just be open to others' views.

Second, welcome contradiction. One of the best ways to combat a destructive tendency is to adopt an "opposite signal" strategy. For example, when you are sad, often the last thing you want to do is see others, but this is precisely what you should do. When your ideas are threatened and you feel defensive, actively reject your instinct to defend yourself and become more open instead. When someone says, "You are wrong," respond with "Tell me more." Make friends who think differently than you and challenge your assumptions—and whose assumptions you challenge. Think of this as building your "team of rivals," the phrase the historian Doris Kearns Goodwin used to describe Abraham Lincoln's cabinet, which, unlike Kennedy's, challenged him relentlessly.[34] If this sounds like torture, it is all the more urgent that you try it.

Third, start small. Let's suppose that you want the benefits of entertaining a friend's point of view. Getting started is hard, especially if the viewpoint is something huge, like your religious beliefs or your political ideology. It's better to start with smaller ideas such as your fashion choices, or even your sports allegiances. Reconsider the things you have long taken for granted, and assess them as dispassionately as you can. Then, with these low stakes, open up to others' views.

The point is not to deal in trivialities. Research on goal setting clearly shows that starting small teaches you how to change and break habits.[35] Then you can scale this self-knowledge up to the bigger areas of your life in which, even if you don't change your views, you can appreciate others'.

If you master these techniques, there might be critics who say you are a flip-flopper, or wishy-washy. To deal with this, take a lesson from the great economist Paul Samuelson, the first American ever to win the Nobel Prize in economics. In 1948, Samuelson published what might be the most celebrated economics textbook of all time.[36] As the years went by and he updated the book, he changed his estimate of the inflation level that was tolerable for the health of the macroeconomy: First, he said 5 percent was acceptable; then, in later editions, 3 percent and 2 percent, prompting the Associated Press to run an article titled "Author Should Make Up His Mind." In a television interview after Samuelson was awarded the Nobel Prize in 1970, he gave his answer to the charge: "When events change, I change my mind. What do you do?"

We bet Samuelson had a lot of close friends.

Challenge 4

MAGICAL THINKING

We often fail to include our romantic partner on our list of friends. They feel kind of like a different species, don't they? Maybe you have had the experience in your life of falling in love with someone but finding down the road that you didn't actually like that person very much. You probably had to unwind a complicated relationship at that point, and maybe it was pretty messy. And you probably puzzled over how could you feel such intense passion for someone you found you didn't even really like as a person.

Passionate love—the early feeling of falling in love—is one of the most powerful and mysterious experiences any of us will face in life. If you feel like your emotions have been hijacked, especially at the beginning, it's because they have been. Your brain looks strikingly like that of someone addicted to drugs, with unusually high activity in brain regions for both pleasure and pain, such as the ventral tegmental area, nucleus accumbens, caudate, insula, dorsal anterior cingulate cortex, and the dorsolateral prefrontal cortex.[37] Meanwhile, your brain has become a chemistry experiment: Physical attraction to another person is indicated by spikes in the sex hormones testosterone and estrogen. Your anticipation of being with your partner and euphoria come from high dopamine and norepinephrine levels.[38] Your uncomfortable infatuation involves a deficit of serotonin.[39] Your attachment and jealousy involve boosts in oxytocin.[40]

Passionate love is you-centric. The neurochemical cocktail in your brain is making you think about your feelings all day long, and about your partner as he or she relates to **you.** So it's no surprise that while exciting, it doesn't bring a lot of happiness.

Passionate love also doesn't last, which people often find disappointing and alarming. When passion recedes, people mistakenly interpret this as love itself receding. Nothing could be further from the truth. The early flush of romantic love must turn into something that is stable and lasting, which is one of the greatest secrets to getting happier. The Harvard Study of Adult Development, which is the longest-running study on individuals over the course of their whole lives, shows that the most important predictor of late-life happiness is stable relationships—especially a long romantic partnership.[41] The healthiest and happiest people at age eighty tend to have been most satisfied in their relationships at age fifty.

The key to successful romance isn't trying to keep passion front and center; it's letting it evolve. This does not mean just sticking together legally: research shows that being married accounts for only 2 percent of subjective well-being later in life.[42] The important thing for well-being is relationship satisfaction, and that depends on what social scientists call "companionate love"—stable affection, mutual understanding, and commitment.[43] Companionate love is a special category of friendship.

You might think companionate love sounds a little, well, dull. This is because our popular culture and media tend to portray love and romance unrealistically, leaning disproportionately on magical thinking like love at first sight and living happily ever after.[44] Research on Disney's animated movies, for example, shows that the majority of them rely on exactly these themes.[45] These films may, in turn, influence children's and young adults' views on romance. A 2002 study on 285 unmarried undergraduate students (both women and men) found a strong correlation between the time they spent watching television programs related to love and romance and how much they expressed idealistic expectations about marriage.[46] A 2016 study found that tween girls who had recently watched a movie depicting a love story were more likely to "endorse idealistic romantic beliefs" than those who had watched a non-romantic movie.[47]

Despite its popularity in stories and movies, love at first sight has little to do with reality. Researchers have found that what people describe as "love at first sight" has no connection to the real hallmarks of true love, including intimacy and commitment.[48] Rather, it is either a phrase people use about the past to romanticize their meeting (notwithstanding the way it actually happened) or one that they use to describe exceptionally strong physical attraction.

Idealistic but unrealistic beliefs can do a lot of damage to your relationship. Take the idea of romantic destiny, or "soul mates"—the belief that two people are deliberately brought together by unseen forces. Research on hundreds of college students has shown that such expectations are correlated with dysfunctional patterns in relationships, such as the assumption that partners will understand and predict each other's wishes and desires with little effort or communication because they're a cosmically perfect match.[49] In other words, a belief in destiny leads to a belief in mind reading.

Companionate love is the right goal—to be the closest of friends, who are also still in love. Passionate love in the early stages is exciting precisely because the other person is a bit of a stranger. Thus, deep friendship is impossible. The goal is to keep attraction alive while getting to know each other intimately.

This intimate friendship means sharing full personhood with each other—to go from "me" to "we." There can obviously be disagreements, anger, and bitterness—even unhappiness. The objective is not to avoid this, but to learn and grow through problems. It is to see them as shared challenges to manage jointly. The goal is **not** to avoid fights; it is to grow closer with a collaborative conflict style (where you work together to find solutions).

Based on the research, there are five ways to develop the deep friendship of companionate love that lasts. First, lighten up. Passionate love tends to be heavy—it is usually serious and unfunny. Good companionate love, which leads to rising happiness, is much lighter, because best friends bring out the lighter side in each other. They gently joke with each other and have fun together. Goof around together, like you do with any close friend.

Second, make the companionate love more about the two of you, and less about each individual. You shouldn't be afraid of arguing, but you have to do it right. Researchers studying couples' arguments have found that those who use "we words" when they fight are apt to have less cardiovascular arousal, fewer negative emotions, and higher marital satisfaction than those who use "me/you words."[50] You might have to work on this, especially if you have built up bad habits over many years. Instead of saying "You don't try to understand my feelings," try "I think we should try to understand each other's feelings." Make **we** your default pronoun when talking with others. If you like staying out late but your partner hates it, say "We prefer not to stay out so late" when you turn down a ten p.m. dinner for your partner's sake.

Third, put your money on your team. Many couples act individualistically when it comes to their money—keeping separate bank accounts, for example. They usually think they are avoiding conflict, and perhaps they are, but they are also avoiding an opportunity to think and act as a team of friends. Indeed, scholars have demonstrated that couples who pool all their money tend to be happier and more likely to stay together.[51] This might be harder for partners with different spending habits, but research has shown that people tend to spend more prudently when they pool their resources.[52]

Fourth, treat your arguments like exercise. Something every inveterate gym-goer will tell you is that if you want to make fitness a long-term habit, you can't view working out as punishment. It will be painful, sure, but you shouldn't be unhappy about doing it regularly, because it makes you stronger. For collaborative couples, conflict can be seen in the same way: it's not fun in the moment, but it is an opportunity to solve inevitable problems collaboratively, which strengthens the relationship.[53] One way to do this is to schedule time to work through an issue, rather than treating it like an emotional emergency. Look at a disagreement as something **we** need to find time to fix, instead of as **me** being attacked by **you,** which is a disturbing emergency.[54]

Finally, make your companionate love exclusive. Romantic love makes most people happiest when it's one-to-one, emotionally and sexually. This isn't popular with some people today, but this life advice is based on evidence, not morality. In 2004, a large survey of American adults found that "the happiness-maximizing number of sexual partners in the previous year is calculated to be 1."[55]

One last point: While companionate romantic love is best when it is exclusive, friendship per se should not be. In 2007, researchers found that married adults who said they had at least two close friends—meaning at least one besides their spouse—had higher levels of life satisfaction and self-esteem and lower levels of depression than spouses who did not have close friends outside their marriage.[56] In other words, long-term companionate love might be necessary, but it isn't sufficient for happiness.

Challenge 5

THE VIRTUAL WORLD

In 1995, Rena Rudavsky and her family were selected to participate in a novel psychology experiment. Researchers at Carnegie Mellon University would install a computer in their dining room and connect it to the internet. At the time, only 9 percent of Americans used the internet (in 2020, nearly 91 percent did).[57] Rena, then a middle schooler, recalled sitting in front of the computer day after day, participating in chat rooms and surfing the internet. When she finished, another family member would take a turn.

Strangely, this experiment didn't spark much discussion in her household. "We did little conversing in the dining room when the computer was on," Rena told us. Furthermore, "none of us shared our private internet experiences with others in our family."

Rena's experience was typical, as the researchers showed when they published the now-famous "HomeNet" study in 1998.[58] "Greater use of the internet was associated with declines in participants' communication with family members in the household" and "declines in the size of their social circle," the researchers wrote. More ominously, it led to "increases in [the participants'] depression and loneliness." Rena says her experience bore out these findings.

HomeNet could be (and has been) interpreted as an indictment of the internet, or screens, or modern communications technology in general. In truth, it illustrates a much simpler truth about love and happiness: technology that crowds out our real-life interaction with others will lower our well-being and thus must be managed with great care in our lives. In order to reap their full benefits, we should use digital tools in ways that enhance our in-person relationships with family and friends.

The coronavirus pandemic prompted a lot of new research on social connection. Anytime the circumstances of social life suddenly change, researchers rush in with our clipboards in hand, asking annoying questions. One of the most common areas of inquiry over the past few years was how the sudden mass shift to digital communication—away from face-to-face—affected overall social connectedness. In one study, researchers surveyed nearly three thousand adults during the pandemic's early months and found that email, social media, online gaming, and texting were inadequate substitutes for in-person interactions.[59] Voice and video calls were somewhat better (although later research also questioned the value of those technologies).[60]

The way solitary diversions such as scrolling or surfing reduce social connection is clear: you do them instead of interacting. Virtual communications such as texting are by design interactive and should theoretically be less harmful; the problem is that with these technologies, we lose **dimensionality.** Text messages can't convey emotion well, because we can't hear or see our interlocutors; the same goes for DMs on social media. (More often, social media is used not to communicate with one individual but to broadcast to a larger audience.) These technologies are to in-person interactions what a black-and-white, pixelated version of the **Mona Lisa** is to the real thing: identifiable, but incapable of producing the same emotional effects.

With low-dimensionality communications, we tend to hop from person to person and thus swap depth for breadth. That's why face-to-face conversations tend to be more expansive than those conducted over text. Research has shown that deeper conversations bring more well-being than short communications.[61] Meanwhile, in a recent longitudinal study, teens who texted more often than their peers tended to experience more depression, more anxiety, more aggression, and poorer relationships with their parents.[62]

It might seem strange that, even outside the circumstances imposed by the pandemic, we would voluntarily adopt technologies that hurt our happiness. There are two major explanations: convenience and presumed courtesy. Vegetating in front of a screen (which nine in ten American teenagers say they do to "pass time") is simply easier than talking with a friend, and virtual communications such as texting are faster and easier than a visit or a phone call.[63] Think of these technologies as grab-and-go food at a convenience store: it's not great, but it sure is easy—and after you eat enough microwave burritos, you forget what the real thing tastes like.

Rena's formative childhood experiment made her think deeply about the internet's effects and has had a lifelong impact on her use of technology. She had a Facebook account in college but deleted it after graduating, and she's never gone back. She avoids other social media networks, and her children have no internet presence. Her work today—which includes, by the way, serving as a research assistant for this book—has a virtual element, but she prefers to go to the office when possible.

By today's standards, her life might sound old-fashioned. Her daughter knocks on neighbors' doors to visit. The family sits on their stoop after dinner, chatting among themselves and with passersby. She writes and sends letters. When she does use technology, it's as a complement to her friendships, not a substitute for them; she maintains a parent text group, for example, but only to set up in-person activities.

For most of us, especially people who grew up with it, the internet is an unquestioned part of the ecosystem of life, seeping into every crack and crevice independent of any conscious decision on our part. We're not going back to life before this kind of technology, of course. We can and should, however, use it mindfully in service of love and friendship. Here are two ways to do so.

First, choose interaction over vegetation. There is nothing revolutionary about this rule—forty-five years ago, kids were told by their parents to go outside with their friends instead of watching television. The difference now, besides the fact that the television didn't fit in my pocket, is empirical evidence: today, we know that, in excess, solitary and screen-based diversion lowers happiness and can lead to mood disorders such as depression and anxiety.[64]

To knock you out of suboptimal habits, make use of device options that inform you of the time you are spending on social media and the internet, and limit yourself to an hour a day or less. Another popular approach, which has not yet been tested in academic research, is turning your devices from color to grayscale.[65]

Second, create a communication hierarchy. It's unreasonable to expect anyone to stop texting, but you can turn to it less if you have an "order of operations" in place for talking with your friends and loved ones. When possible, make an effort to meet in person—especially with your intimates. A 2021 study revealed that the more face-to-face communication people had with others, the more understood they felt and the more satisfied they were with their relationship.[66] When meeting up is impossible, use face-to-face technology or the phone. Text or use similar technology for only impersonal or urgent matters.

THE BLISSFUL WORK OF FRIENDSHIP

Friendship is incorrectly seen by many people as something that just occurs naturally, without conscious effort or work. This is false; like everything else important, friendship requires attention and work. It must be built on purpose. The big challenges we have covered in this chapter can become opportunities by remembering five lessons.

1. Don't let an introverted personality or a fear of rejection block your ability to make friends, and don't let extroversion prevent you from going deep.
2. Friendship is ruined when we look for people who are useful to us for reasons other than friendship itself. Build links that are based on

love and enjoyment of another's company, not what she or he can do for you professionally or socially.

3. Too many deep friendships today are spoiled by differences of opinion. Love for others can be enhanced, not harmed, by differences, if we elect to show humility instead of pride—and the happiness benefits are enormous.

4. The goal for long-term romance is a special kind of friendship, not undying passion. Companionate love is based on trust and mutual affection, and is what old people who still love each other talk about.

5. Real friendship requires real contact. Technology can complement your deepest relationships, but it is a terrible substitute. Look for more ways to be together in person with the people you love the most.

The first two pillars on which to build a happier life—family and friendship—require a lot of time and commitment. For many people, however, a lot more time is spent doing something else: working. If you work forty hours a week and commute on top of that, this might be the single most time-consuming activity in your life. With this kind of investment, even if it is less important to you than your family and friend relationships, happiness will be hard to increase if work is a source of misery.

But "not being a source of misery" is hardly the kind of goal we should shoot for—we can and should do much better. Work should bring happiness benefits beyond just giving us the resources we need to survive and support our families. And that is our next topic: making earning our daily bread a source of joy.

Seven

Work That Is Love Made Visible

The third pillar for building a happier life is meaningful work. Hundreds of studies have shown that job satisfaction and life satisfaction are positively related, and causal: liking your job causes you to be happier all around.[1] Engaging in work with your whole heart is one of the best ways to enjoy your days, get satisfaction from your accomplishments, and see meaning in your efforts. Work, at its best, is "love made visible," in the elegant words of the Lebanese poet Kahlil Gibran.[2]

That's the good news. It's also the bad news. When your work is drudgery, it is bereft of love, and can make life a task. There's no joy in dragging yourself out of bed in the morning to go to a job you hate—where you feel helpless, bored, or unappreciated. Some jobs really are objectively miserable. And striving simply to squeeze by financially is stressful under the best of circumstances. But for most people, when they learn that getting happier starts within, they can make work less stressful, more joyful, and a source of personal growth.

It would be convenient if we could tell you exactly what the right job is to do that, and how to get it. But work that raises your happiness does **not** mean finding a specific job with a lot of prestige or income (although we all have to make enough money to get by). You can love or hate being a lawyer, an electrician, a homemaker, or a full-time volunteer. Researchers who have looked for clear relationships between job satisfaction and the actual type of job one holds have overwhelmingly struck out. In a 2018 survey, the "happiest jobs" had nothing in common: teaching assistant, quality-assurance analyst, net developer, and marketing specialist.[3] The unhappiest jobs are similarly grab-baggy, and fairly unrelated to education and income: accountant, security guard, cashier, and supervisor.

Consider the following two cases that illustrate that happiness depends on **you,** not your specific job.

Stephanie's dream since college was to lead the top company in her industry as CEO. She worked and strove, and in her midforties, she made it to the corner office. And when she made it, she succeeded spectacularly in the job. She took her company to new heights financially and was popular internally.

She got positive press for her leadership, and she made good money.

"I got the brass ring," she said, "and I'm proud of that." But there were sacrifices. "I missed a lot of my kids' childhood," she admitted. "And it hurt my marriage a lot to be gone so much of the time." She also conceded that while she knew a huge number of people and had hundreds of friends, none of them were real friends—mostly just clients and colleagues.

After more than a decade of bone-crushing work and top performance, Stephanie was exhausted. Her board and employees would have gladly seen her stay many more years—after all, things were going great for the company—but being honest with herself, she had to conclude that her life simply wasn't passing the cost-benefit test for happiness. There were nice times, but they were smothered in stress. And she felt profoundly alone.

Even the legacy Stephanie thought she was building was an illusion. She went back to visit her company a few months after resigning, walking into an opulent headquarters erected during her tenure, and it was as if she had been erased. There was no bad blood, just . . . forward motion. The new CEO was traveling the same routes she had, meeting the same clients, doing the same deals. Her old colleagues were cordial and friendly, but almost no one was especially interested in what she was up to now. "Why would they be?" she asked rhetorically. Today, she is retired from executive work at fifty-nine, congratulated by all for her "success," but still looking for something to help make her feel fully alive.

Now consider Alex. His dreams were more modest than Stephanie's. He was raised in a middle-class family with middle-class expectations: he would get decent grades, go to a state university, and start a career that offered security—a plausible and rational formula to live a good life. For some reason, that formula never fit Alex, though. He was a solid B student in high school but was never sparked by any of his classes. He went right to college, where he studied accounting, but for him, that was sheer drudgery.

After college, Alex landed a job in the accounting office of a manufacturing company in his hometown. He worked there for a year and then moved to another job that paid slightly more. Over the next two decades he traded up every few years, and by his midforties was making a decent (but not spectacular) living. The bright spot in his life was his family and friends. He was happily married, had three kids, and had close friends from high school whom he saw most weekends. He also loved cars and enjoyed keeping his in immaculate condition.

Alex says that during this period, he figured that everyone disliked work and did it only out of sheer necessity. Every day at the office was a grueling marathon for him. The paperwork bored him, and he couldn't stand looking out his office window at the parking lot. He was grateful for a steady job that allowed him to help support his family, but he spent every day watching the clock move in slow motion toward five p.m., when he could go home.

One day, at age forty-five, Alex was complaining after dinner to his wife for the millionth time about his job. Half listening, she asked him, "Is there anything that you do every day that you actually enjoy?" He thought about it, and could come up with only two amusingly mundane activities: "I like driving to work, and I like talking to people on my breaks."

"So why don't you quit and become an Uber driver?" she joked. Boom. What was meant as a joke was like Alex's road-to-Damascus moment. He did it, and has been driving for a living for the past five years.

"I actually work more hours and make slightly less money than I did," he said. "But I look forward to work. I meet new and interesting people and get to drive all day." He said he comes home in a good mood and never worries about work problems. All that makes him a better husband and father. "I am twice as happy as I used to be," he reported.

These are both true stories, not made-up examples. Only the names and a few details have been changed to protect the anonymity of the subjects.

Don't misunderstand: There is nothing in these two stories to suggest that either Stephanie or Alex got a bad deal in life or made irrational choices. Nor is it the case that making it to CEO or driving for a living inherently brings more happiness or unhappiness than the other. Maybe running a company would be a blast for you, and driving others around would be awful—or vice versa. The fanciest job can be a disappointment or a triumph, and an "ordinary" job with moderate pay can be delightful or terrible. The decision to stay home to raise your kids, if you can afford it, can be wonderful—or not. Retirement can raise your happiness or lower it.

To build a career that makes you happier means understanding yourself. It means being the boss of your own life, even if you aren't technically the boss at work. Doing so means managing four big challenges—which Alex overcame, leading to much greater happiness, but Stephanie didn't.

Challenge 1

CAREER GOALS

You might be a person who absolutely loves her or his work, has a completely healthy work-life balance, and can't think of anything that could make this part of life better. Wait . . . you're **not**?

In truth, most people are more or less OK with their jobs, but don't see them as an enormous source of satisfaction. They don't know how to make things a lot better, though, and thus leave this part of life "good enough." In 2022, for example, just 16 percent of employees were "very satisfied" with their work.[4] Thirty-seven percent were "somewhat satisfied." Everyone else said they were "somewhat dissatisfied" or "very dissatisfied," or said, "I am just glad to have a job." How would you answer?

The way to make this better, like Alex did, is to start by clarifying your goals. If your answer to the preceding question was "I am just glad to have a job," you might be motivated by trying to avoid unemployment, the threat of which is one of the biggest sources of unhappiness people can face. American adults who reported that they were "very" or "fairly" likely to lose their job in 2018 were more than three times as likely to say they were "not too happy" with their life as people who felt they were "not likely" to be let go.[5] In 2014, economists found that a one-percentage-point increase in unemployment lowers national well-being by more than five times as much as a one-point increase in the inflation rate.[6]

If you aren't in real danger of unemployment, you can set your sights higher. As social scientists would note, while pay and benefits are **necessary,** they aren't **sufficient.** Pay and benefits are like eating and sleeping are for your health. You absolutely need them, and if you mess around with them too much, bad things will happen, but if you make these things your only focus, you will wind up unhealthy and unhappy.

Your pay and benefits are what are called extrinsic rewards. These come from the outside. If you are someone who has a high-power, high-prestige job, that would also fall into this category. Meanwhile, your job also has intrinsic rewards, which come from inside you—the inherent fulfillment and enjoyment you get when you do your work. You need extrinsic rewards to get by, but you need intrinsic rewards to get happier.

In a classic 1973 study on extrinsic and intrinsic rewards, researchers at Stanford and the University of Michigan allowed a group of kids to choose their preferred play activities—for example, drawing with markers—which they happily did for fun (intrinsic rewards).[7] The kids were later rewarded for that activity with a certificate featuring a gold seal and a ribbon (extrinsic rewards). The researchers found that after they had been given the certificate, the children became only about half as likely to want to draw as when they weren't offered one. Over the following decades, many studies have shown the same pattern for a wide variety of activities, across many demographic groups.[8]

We humans have a funny tendency to value what we are doing in terms of what people are giving us to do it. If someone pays us, it must be onerous—otherwise they wouldn't need to. That's why the satisfaction in the experiments falls when the scientists introduce compensation. This is obviously not to say that we should all work for free; rather, it is simply to point out that for happiness, our goals shouldn't be just to maximize extrinsic rewards. We should also consciously keep intrinsic goals front and center.

So how do we set goals to achieve intrinsic rewards at work while we make a living? One answer might be to try and find a job that follows the advice of commencement speakers, who always seem to say, "Find a job you love and you'll never work a day in your life." This sounds like the right intrinsic reward is to have a job that is a total blast every day.

We've never seen that job in real life. Furthermore, you might be a little suspicious of that advice, given that it always seems to come from unbelievably successful people, who, if you look into their backgrounds, absolutely killed themselves early in their careers, often paying an enormous personal price in their relationships to get to the top. They certainly didn't take their own advice.

Obviously, you shouldn't sign up for something you hate, but the right intrinsic reward isn't "super fun every day." Looking for that will put you on another El Dorado quest for something that doesn't exist, and lead to frustration. Rather than relentlessly pursuing a "perfect match" career, a better approach is to remain flexible on the exact job, while searching for two big things.

The first is **earned success.** You can think of it as the opposite of learned helplessness, a term coined by the psychologist Martin Seligman to denote the resignation that people experience when they repeatedly endure unpleasant situations beyond their control.[9] Earned success instead gives you a sense of accomplishment and professional efficacy (the idea that you are effective in your job, which pushes up commitment to your occupation, which is also a good measure of job satisfaction).[10]

The best way to enjoy earned success is to find ways to get better at your job, whether that leads to promotions and higher pay or not. Obviously, having work where extrinsic rewards follow is great. Employers who give clear guidance and feedback, reward merit, and encourage their employees to develop new skills are the best employers. Even if you aren't in a job with that kind of extrinsic reward, set excellence goals for yourself, such as "I will make each of my customers feel special today."

And this leads to the second, related intrinsic goal, which is **service to others**—the sense that your job is making the world a better place. That doesn't mean you need to volunteer or work for a charity to be happy (research has shown that nonprofit work is not more inherently satisfying than working for a for-profit or for the government).[11] On the contrary, you can find service in almost any job.

One young man made this point perfectly, in an op-ed he wrote to explain why, despite holding an MBA, he had chosen to become a waiter in a restaurant in Barcelona.[12] As he put it, his customers "are all important and equal. They are the same at the table and must be the same in the eyes of the waiter. . . . It's great to be able to serve the politician on the front page of the newspaper just as well as the kid browsing the news while waiting for his girlfriend." This young man needed extrinsic rewards to make a living, but he didn't choose to maximize them to the exclusion of his intrinsic rewards.

Earned success and service to others are easier in some jobs than in others. If, for example, you are in a profession you think is hurting others, service will be hard to achieve. That's why a good rule of thumb is to look for a fundamental match between an employer's values and your own. When people believe in the mission of their employer, they have a lot of intrinsic motivation for their work.[13] This is especially true when the values have special moral, philosophical, or spiritual significance, and it holds even when a job is exhausting and hard. For example, a 2012 study on nurses found that the happiest ones believed their work was "a divine profession and a tool by which they could gain spiritual pleasure and satisfaction."[14]

We know perfectly well that these goals aren't always easy, and even in the best cases, they can be very elusive on certain days. Even if you find the employer you believe in, that rewards your merit, and where you are serving people all day, you will come home from work some days unfulfilled and frustrated. Think of it like being in a sailboat. You know the wind will blow you off course pretty regularly, but if you have the right coordinates, you will always be able to reorient yourself.

Challenge 2

CAREER PATH

Relying on extrinsic rewards lowers satisfaction. It can even lock you into the wrong career trajectory for decades to come. This is because it makes you pursue a career path that is wrong for you.

Whether you make a lot of money or just a little, the world tells you that there is really just one responsible type of career path: you select a career, you find a job, and you change jobs only when something better in your field comes along. Let's say you come out of high school and take a job as a receptionist at a law firm. You don't just walk away when it's boring or stressful; you stay with it until someone hires you away with a better job. It's the same system whether you are a college professor or a talk show host. You stay with one job until something fancier that pays better comes along. This is what psychologists call the "linear" career model.[15]

It makes a lot of sense for some people, but it is a huge problem for others. Maybe you have a lot of different interests that you would like to pursue, and you think going back to school for a new career would be interesting and fun. Or you highly value a lifestyle where you're good at what you do, but you do not want to work long hours, even if that means not advancing in your career. A linear path doesn't allow for these preferences. Maybe you are a highly educated woman with a great job, but you want to stay home when your kids are born. The linear career says, "Sorry, you can't do that."

Fortunately, there are three other career models. "Steady-state" careers are those that are associated with one job over decades, where one doesn't advance much but increases in expertise. This is common for people who value job security a lot but don't want to bust their hump every day to get ahead. This was much more common in the past than it is today. However, it might be right for you if you really love stability and want a job that, while it doesn't make you rich, is financially secure and allows you to spend your life on things you care a lot about outside work.

Another model is the "transitory" career, which jumps around all over the place. From the outside it looks chaotic: You were waiting tables in Denver, and now you are working for a moving company in Tucson. In a few years you might be driving a long-haul truck out of Seattle. This isn't chaos, however; it is the profile of someone who loves trying new things, and who moves around based on non-job criteria, such as lifestyle, location, or social life.

"Spiral" careers are the last category. This is like a series of smaller careers. People in this model might make a pretty dramatic career shift every decade or so, but there is a method to the madness. They are using their skills and knowledge in one field and applying it to another, while getting a variety of experiences for their own fulfillment. So, for example, you might work out of college for a decade doing something connected to what you studied. Then, you might decrease your pay by using your skills in another field. Or you might start your own business. Or maybe you take ten years away from the workforce to raise your children, and return to something completely different.

So, you might be asking, which is the right path for you? In your heart, you probably know already. One of the models we just described made you feel excited and maybe a little scared. Another deadened you inside. And in general, this is the way to know how to proceed along the professional path of your life. Always follow the signals that you yourself are producing internally—and that may be uncomfortable. When you are thinking about a professional opportunity, take some quiet time over a few days or weeks to imagine the job or career in detail. Then, discern how it makes you feel. Does this opportunity **excite** you, **frighten** you, or **deaden** you?

Say, for example, you are offered a job in the management of your company. You enjoy your current job and like your colleagues, and worry that a big promotion will make you enjoy your work less and hurt your work-life balance. But it is a great opportunity, and significantly more money. Almost everyone is encouraging you to take it. If it excites you a lot and frightens you a little, this is a signal to move forward. If it simply frightens you, you need a lot more information. If it deadens you when you imagine doing the new job, the answer is clear: turn it down.

Challenge 3

ADDICTION

If you have figured out the right objectives and found your professional path, congratulations—but you aren't yet in the clear in building this part of your life. In fact, there are a number of hazards you need to be aware of that specifically afflict hard-working people of high ambition. The first is the tendency toward workaholism, which people engage in to distract themselves from pain in their lives. This leaves the root problems unaddressed, and even makes them worse by harming family relationships.

Consider the case of Winston Churchill, the statesman, soldier, and writer. He was one of the first world leaders to sound the alarm about the Nazi menace in the 1930s, and then he captivated the global imagination as a leader against the Axis powers in World War II. While prime minister of the United Kingdom during the war, he kept a crushing schedule, often spending eighteen hours a day at work. On top of this, he wrote book after book while in office. By the end of his life, he had finished forty-three, filling seventy-two volumes.[16]

You probably admire Churchill, and for good reason, but you shouldn't envy him. He suffered from crippling depression, which he called his "black dog" and which visited him again and again. He once told his doctor, "I don't like to stand by the side of a ship and look down into the water. A second's action would end everything."[17]

It seems almost unbelievable that Churchill could be so productive while in such a dark place. Some say his depression was bipolar, and windows of mania allowed him to work as much as he did. A few of his biographers explain it differently: Churchill's workaholism wasn't in spite of his suffering, but in part **because of** it.[18] He distracted himself from his problems with work. Lest you think this far-fetched, researchers today find that workaholism is a common addiction in response to emotional distress. And like so many addictions, it worsens the situation it's meant to alleviate.

In 2018, researchers analyzed a decade's worth of data and found that 24 percent of people with an anxiety disorder and nearly 22 percent of people with a mood disorder (such as major depression or bipolar disorder) self-medicate using alcohol or drugs.[19] Self-medicators were far more likely to develop substance dependence. For example, epidemiological data revealed that people who self-medicated for anxiety using alcohol were more than six times as likely to develop persistent alcohol dependence as those who didn't self-medicate.[20]

There is compelling evidence that some people treat their emotional problems with work as well. This can lead to its own kind of addiction. Many studies have shown a strong association between workaholism and the symptoms of psychiatric disorders, such as anxiety and depression, and it has been common to assume that compulsive work leads to these maladies.[21] But some psychologists have recently argued reverse causation—that people may treat their depression and anxiety with workaholic behavior.[22] As the authors of one widely reported 2016 study wrote, "Workaholism (in some instances) develops as an attempt to reduce uncomfortable feelings of anxiety and depression."[23]

This might explain why so many people increased their work hours during the COVID pandemic.[24] For many months during the initial shutdowns, people faced boredom, loneliness, and anxiety; by late May 2020, the US Centers for Disease Control data showed that nearly a quarter of American adults had reported symptoms of depression.[25] (In 2019, that figure was 6.5 percent.) Perhaps a portion of workers self-treated by doubling down on their jobs in order to feel busy and productive.

People who struggle with workaholism can easily deny that it's a problem, and thus miss the underlying issues they are self-treating. How can work be bad? As the Stanford psychiatrist Anna Lembke, the author of **Dopamine Nation: Finding Balance in the Age of Indulgence,** put it, "Even previously healthy and adaptive behaviors—behaviors that I think we broadly as a culture would think of as healthy, advantageous behaviors—now have become drugified such that they are made more potent, more accessible, more novel, more ubiquitous."[26] If you are sneaking into the bathroom at home to check your work email on your iPhone, she's talking about you.

What's more, when it comes to work, people reward you for addictive behavior. No one says, "Wow, an entire bottle of gin in one night? You are an outstanding drinker." But work sixteen hours a day and you'll probably get a promotion.

Despite the extolled virtues of maximum work, the costs will almost certainly outrun the benefits, as they usually do in self-medicating addictions. The burnout, depression, job stress, and work-life conflict will get worse, not better.[27] And as Lembke also noted, workaholism can lead to secondary addictions, such as to drugs, alcohol, or pornography, which people use to self-medicate for the problems caused by the primary addiction, often with catastrophic personal consequences.

There are solutions to work addiction, according to Harvard professor Ashley Whillans.[28] She recommends three practices, starting with a "time audit." For a few days, keep a careful log of your major activities—work, leisure, running errands—as well as how long you spent on each one and how you felt. Note the activities that bring you the most positive mood and meaning. This will give you two pieces of information: how much you are working (to make denial impossible), and what you like to do when you aren't working (to make recovery more attractive).

Next, Professor Whillans recommends scheduling your downtime. Workaholics tend to marginalize nonwork activities as "nice to have," and thus crowd them out with work. This is how the fourteenth hour of work, which is rarely productive, displaces an hour you might have spent with your children. Block off time in your day for nonwork activities, just as you do for meetings.

Finally, program your leisure. Don't leave those downtime slots too loose. Unstructured time is an invitation to turn back to work, or to passive activities that aren't great for well-being, such as scrolling social media or watching television. You probably have a to-do list that is organized in priority order. Do the same with your leisure, planning active pastimes you value. If you enjoy calling your friend, don't leave it for when you happen to have time—schedule it and stick to the plan. Treat your walks, prayer time, and gym sessions as if they were meetings with the president.

Dealing with a work addiction can make a real difference in our lives. It opens up time for family and friends. It allows nonwork pastimes that are not useful, just fun. It enables us to take better care of ourselves, for example, by exercising. All of these things have been shown to raise happiness or lower unhappiness.

Addressing workaholism still leaves the underlying issue that working so hard was meant to treat. Perhaps you, too, are visited by Churchill's black dog. Or maybe your dog is a different color: a troubled marriage; a chronic sense of inadequacy; maybe even ADHD or obsessive-compulsive disorder, which have been linked to overwork.[29] Ceasing to use work to distract yourself from that is an opportunity to face your troubles, perhaps with help, and thus solve the problem that got you hooked on excessive work in the first place.

Facing the dog might seem scarier than simply turning to the old dogcatchers: your boss, your colleagues, your career. Unlike Churchill, you might just find a way to get rid of that mutt for good.

Challenge 4

IDENTITY

If you are on a linear, steady-state, transitory, or spiral career path, the odds are that you care a lot about your work. When people ask you what you do, you enthusiastically tell them about your profession. In many ways, your job is a huge part of your identity. This tends to be particularly true for people interested in self-improvement.

There's nothing wrong with identifying strongly with your profession and being proud of your work. Professional excellence is a great virtue, and we have sought mightily to be excellent in what we do for a living, too. But there's a danger lurking here. It is all too easy to lose your true self to a representation of yourself that is your job title or duties. You aren't Mary, mother of three, or John, devoted husband; first and foremost you are Mary, regional manager, or John, senior teacher. This is what is called **self-objectification.**

Objectification of other people is obviously problematic. Research shows that when people are reduced by others to, for example, physical attributes through objectifying stares or harassment, it can lower self-confidence and ability in tasks.[30] The philosopher Immanuel Kant referred to this as becoming "an Object of appetite for another," at which point "all motives of moral relationship cease to function."[31]

Physical objectification is just one type. Objectification at work is another, and an especially dangerous one. In 2021, researchers measured workplace objectification. They found that it led to burnout, unhappiness with one's job, and depression.[32] This can happen if a boss treats her employees like nothing more than disposable labor, or even if employees see their boss as nothing more than a provider of money.

So it's pretty easy to see why we shouldn't objectify others. Less obvious but equally damaging is when the objectifier and the person being objectified are one and the same—when you objectify yourself. Humans are capable of objectifying themselves in many ways—by assessing their self-worth in terms of their physical appearance, economic position, or political views, for example—but all of them boil down to one damaging core act: reducing your own humanity to a single characteristic, thus encouraging others to do so as well. In the case of work, that might mean deciding on your own self-worth based on your pay or prestige.

Just as social media encourages us to self-objectify physically, our work culture pushes us to self-objectify professionally. Americans tend to admire people who are busy and ambitious, so letting work take over virtually every moment of your life is easy. We know many people who talk of almost nothing besides their work, who are saying, essentially, "I am my job." This may feel more humanizing and empowering than saying, "I am my boss's tool," but that reasoning has a fatal flaw: In theory, you can ditch your boss and get a new job. You can't ditch **you.** Remember: **You are your own CEO.**

Self-objectification at work is a tyranny. We become a terrible boss to ourselves, with little mercy or love. Days off provoke guilt and a sense of laziness, which is a way we condemn and belittle ourselves. To the question "Am I successful enough yet?" the answer is always "No—work harder!" And then, when the end inevitably comes, when professional decline sets in or we have a setback to our careers, we are left bereft and desiccated.

Are you a self-objectifier in your job or career? If you answered affirmatively, recognize that you will never be satisfied as long as you objectify yourself. Your career or job should be an extension of you, not vice versa. Two practices can help as you reassess your priorities.

First, put some space between your job and your life. Maybe you have been in an unhealthy relationship or two in your life but only recognized this when you had a break from it, whether voluntary or involuntary. Indeed, this human tendency probably contributes to the fact that most trial separations lead to divorce, especially when they last more than a year.[33] Space provides perspective.

Use this principle in your professional life. To begin with, the main goal of your vacation should be to get a break from work and spend time with people you love. As obvious as this may sound, that means **taking your vacation,** and not working during it at all. Your employer should thank you for doing so, because people are better workers when they are refreshed.

Related to this is the ancient idea of Sabbath-keeping, or taking regular time away from work each week. In religious traditions, rest isn't just nice to have; it is central to understanding God and ourselves. "For in six days the Lord made heaven and earth, the sea, and all that is in them, and rested on the seventh day," the book of Exodus instructs. "Therefore the Lord blessed the Sabbath day and made it holy." If God rests from work, maybe you should, too.

Such a practice doesn't have to be religious, and it can be done in a lot of ways besides simply avoiding all work on Saturday or Sunday.[34] For example, you can take a small Sabbath each evening by avoiding work and dedicating all your activity to relationships and leisure. (That means no checking your work email.)

Make some friends who don't see you as a professional object. Many professional self-objectifiers seek out others who admire them solely for their work accomplishments. This is quite natural, but it can easily become a barrier to the formation of real friendships, which we all need. By self-objectifying in your friendships, you can make it easier for your friends to objectify you.

This is why having friends outside your professional circles is so important. Striking up friendships with people who don't have any connection to your professional life encourages you to develop nonwork interests and virtues, and thus be a fuller person. The way to do this goes hand in hand with recommendation number one: Don't just spend time away from work; spend it with people who have no connection to your work. (If your job is taking care of your family, this principle still applies. You need to have relationships with people who see you as more than a provider and caretaker.)

Maybe challenging your self-objectification makes you feel uneasy. The reason is simple: we all want to stand out in some way, and working harder than others and being better at our jobs seems a straightforward way to do so. This is a normal human drive, but it can nonetheless lead to destructive ends.[35] Many successful people confess that they would rather be special than happy.[36]

The great irony is that by trying to be special, we end up reducing ourselves to a single quality and turning ourselves into cogs in a machine of our own making. In the famous Greek myth, Narcissus fell in love not with himself, but with the image of himself. And so it is when we professionally self-objectify: we learn to love the image of our successful selves, not ourselves as we truly are in life.

Don't make this mistake. You are not your job, and we are not ours. Take your eyes off the distorted reflection, and have the courage to experience your full life and true self.

LOVE MADE VISIBLE

When it comes to building the life you want, you need to get the work part of your life right. Think about it: probably a **third of your life** will be spent working—whether that is formal employment, taking care of your family, or some other arrangement.

As you examine your vocation and contemplate changes, keep in mind the four challenges in this chapter, and the lessons that help you turn them into great opportunities to grow in happiness.

1. Seek intrinsic rewards from your work. The right goals to get the greatest satisfaction from work are not money and power, but rather, earned success and service to others. Seek these and you will build a work life that consistently brings joy to you and others.
2. There is not just one path to career success and happiness. Figure out if you are linear, steady state, transitory, or spiral. Then pursue that path by paying attention to your internal signals.
3. Work addiction is no joke for many millions of Americans and others all around the world. Look honestly at your own patterns and assess the health of your habits.

4. You are not your job. Self-objectification will lead to unhappiness. Make sure you get space from your work, and have people in your life who see you as a person, not as just a professional.

Once again, we simply cannot tell anyone what specific job will bring the greatest happiness. It depends on you. What all happy jobs have in common is that for you, the work is something better than just a means to a physical end. That is why we titled this chapter "Work That Is Love Made Visible."

This can be a tall order. There are days when your work doesn't feel like love made visible, invisible, or anything else. The trick isn't arriving at some far-off state of perfection, it is working toward getting better. To get happier, you strive toward the goal of making your work meaningful.

For people of a spiritual or religious inclination, the trick can be to join your physical labor to the metaphysical. This was the fundamental philosophy of the Spanish Catholic saint Josemaría Escrivá. As he argued, through our work we passionately love the world:

> [God] waits for us every day, in the laboratory, in the operating theatre, in the army barracks, in the university chair, in the factory, in the workshop, in the fields, in the

> home and in all the immense panorama of work. Understand this well: there is something holy, something divine hidden in the most ordinary situations, and it is up to each one of you to discover it.[37]

Perhaps you read these words and marvel that anyone could find sacredness in the mundanity of a job like yours—or any part of ordinary life. It can be done, and you can do it, whether you are traditionally religious or not. But that requires an understanding of the next pillar for building the life you want: **finding your path to the transcendent.**

Eight

Find Your Amazing Grace

"Amazing Grace" is the most popular Christian hymn ever written, and has been recorded more than seven thousand times.[1] You certainly know the tune, and probably even the words of the first verse by heart.

> **Amazing grace, how sweet the sound**
> **That saved a wretch like me**
> **I once was lost, but now I'm found**
> **Was blind but now I see.**

What you may not know is the story behind this famous hymn, written around 1772 by a British man by the name of John Newton. Newton was forty-seven when he wrote it, after having led a life—as he later characterized it—of dissipation and sin, bereft of religious conviction and moral principles.[2] He made his living transporting enslaved people, after having himself fled forced enlistment in the British Royal Navy.

One night when Newton was aboard a ship returning to London, a storm broke out that swept many of his mates out to sea and nearly did the same to him. Later, pondering the reason for his survival, he concluded it was the hand of God, that there was a plan for his life, and his job was to discover it. His habits and beliefs changed as he turned his focus to divine love. He married, and he ultimately became a clergyman and an ardent abolitionist against slavery. Today he is considered one of the people most responsible for the legal end of that institution in Britain.

Newton's faith was, he believed, what made him truly free for the first time in his life. He certainly isn't the first person to assert this. However, his famous hymn makes two striking claims. First, he didn't find his faith; he was **found.** And his happiness didn't come from blocking out the truths of life. On the contrary, his happiness came only when he was able to finally **see** the truth.

Here's the bold claim made in that famous hymn: a search for transcendent truth—in Newton's case, in the Christian religion; more broadly, in something beyond the here and now—illuminates life. It allows you to actually **see reality.** And this leads to a new kind of joy unavailable from any other source.

How absurd, some might respond. To see reality, we should focus on the unseen and unproven? Reason requires faith? This is like saying that fire requires water, or light requires darkness.

In fact, the science is crystal clear. Transcendental beliefs and experiences aid dramatically in our efforts to get happier. Why? Left to our devices, we always focus on the details of our individual lives. This is only natural. Our attention is occupied by our job, our home, our money, our social media accounts, our lunch, and on and on. Most of this is not unimportant, but if we focus only on ourselves and our narrow interests, it gets, well, **tedious.** We lose a perspective on life.

Following a metaphysical path allows us to get a more accurate perspective on life by zooming out on our quotidian worries and everyday cares. It makes us happier by taking the focus off ourselves and putting it instead on the majesties of the universe. It also makes us kinder and more generous toward others—less obsessed with getting and keeping things for ourselves and more in tune with the needs of a world in which we are but one part. Most important, the path of transcendence is an adventure, a spiritual expedition that can add a kind of excitement to our lives beyond anything else we have ever experienced.

But the world—and our emotions—holds us back. People are shamed by the claim that the interior life is unscientific, that the lack of proof of things unseen is evidence that transcendental beliefs are nothing more than a form of superstition. They wither under a culture that denigrates faith and spirituality at every turn. And they find their own doubts overwhelming—they just don't **feel** it often enough, and conclude that it is silly.

In truth, as you will see in this chapter, spiritual experiences have a deep scientific basis to them, and transcendental experiences provide us with important information about life we cannot get in any other way. Getting these experiences, however, takes effort and commitment. The challenges we all generally face in doing so—and the solutions—make up this chapter.

Writing about Faith Is Tricky

For the two of us, spirituality and faith are central to our lives. We have no intention in this chapter of trying to convert you to any specific beliefs, including our own, but we should begin by disclosing what we believe so you can read this chapter with this information in mind.

Arthur: My faith is the most important part of my life. I was raised as a Protestant, but converted to Catholicism as a teenager, after having a

---

mystical experience at the Shrine of Our Lady of Guadalupe in Mexico City. (My parents weren't thrilled, but figured that as adolescent rebellion goes, that was probably better than drugs.) My practice has steadily grown over my adulthood, especially as I have specialized in studying happiness. Today, I attend Mass daily and pray the rosary—an ancient Catholic meditative prayer—each evening with my wife, Ester.

Despite my deep Christian beliefs and practices, I am a serious student of other traditions in both the West and the East, and am close with leaders of many faiths. I have worked with Hindu, Buddhist, Muslim, and Jewish scholars who have brought me closer to God, taught me many truths, improved my faith practices, and enriched my soul. I have also taken a great deal into my beliefs from secular philosophies such as Stoicism.

Oprah: I have been guided by a divine hand my whole life. I call that hand God. I practice and honor the Christian faith but remain open to the mystery of all connections, to the oneness we all share coming from the source of all existence. In the words of the theologian and philosopher Pierre Teilhard de Chardin, I believe we're spiritual beings having this human experience, and we're all somehow linked to each other in nature, in what I think of as Life.

On my **Super Soul** television show and podcasts, I've interviewed hundreds of spiritual teachers and thought leaders from every religion and no religion, and they all emphasize that the spiritual path is the ultimate journey. What I've observed over thousands of conversations is that Life is always speaking to us, trying to urge us toward the best version of ourselves. For me, having a spiritual practice has provided an accelerated route to building the life I want.

We both have tremendous love and appreciation for people of all faiths—and no faith—who are sincerely trying to lift others up and make the world better for all people. Again, our objective in this chapter is **not** to convince you of the rightness of our specific beliefs and practices. Rather, it is to show you how pursuing insight into the transcendent and metaphysical aspects of your life can enrich your existence immeasurably, and help others as well.

YOUR SPIRITUAL BRAIN

Why do religious and spiritual people practice? Ask them and they will rarely say, "So I can be happier." Rather, they will most likely tell you, like John Newton, that it allows them to make sense of their lives in a confusing world. They have found that insight is not available through their ordinary routines, or through worldly distractions such as entertainment and consumption. Many seek a source of experiences that are "bigger" than what daily life can provide, such as a sense of awe, a feeling of oneness with others or the divine, and a loss of the boundaries of space and time.

This is not all fun and games. People report intense discomfort when adopting a transcendental practice because it shines a bright light on themselves. Beginning meditators have often never been alone with their thoughts. Converts to many religions must confront their sins. Studying the philosophers and applying their insights to life involves fear and sacrifice. To follow almost any spiritual practice is to say, "I am going to admit I don't know everything and do this hard thing that the world says is weird and silly."

The result tends to be life-changing, starting with our physiology. The psychologist Lisa Miller, author of the book **The Awakened Brain,** has done extensive work with her colleagues on the neurological mechanisms of transcendent experiences. She has found, for example, that compared with remembering a stressful experience, remembering a spiritual experience reduces activity in the medial thalamus and caudate—the brain regions associated with sensory and emotional processing—thus, perhaps, helping people escape the virtual prison of overthinking and rumination.[3] By studying behavior in patients with brain lesions, other scholars have linked self-reported spirituality to activity in the periaqueductal gray, the brain-stem region associated with (among other things) the moderation of fear and pain, and feelings of love.[4]

Memories of especially strong spiritual encounters—such as, for example, union with God—have been observed using electroencephalogram technology. In one experiment on Carmelite Catholic nuns, neuroscientists in 2008 compared the sisters' brain activity when they were instructed to recall the most mystical experience of their lives versus when they were asked to remember their most intense state of union with another person.[5] The mystical condition (compared with the control condition) induced a significant increase in theta waves in the brain, a pattern also associated with dreaming.[6] In follow-up interviews, the nuns spoke of feeling God's presence during the original experiences, as well as unconditional and infinite love.

Religious belief is strongly correlated with searching for—and finding—purpose in life. Psychologists writing in 2017 measured 442 people's stated level of religious commitment, and found it strongly correlated with their sense of meaning.[7] Perhaps not surprisingly, given the strong association between having a sense of meaning and happiness, religion and spirituality have been shown to protect against depression recurrence and anxious reactions to mistakes.[8]

Researchers have shown the same pattern for physical ailments. Patients undergoing treatment of serious illness reported better quality of life if spiritual-care professionals (such as chaplains) were involved in their care along with doctors and nurses, compared with those whose spiritual needs were left out of their care plans.[9]

Religion and spirituality pursued in community with others can also lower people's sense of isolation. This might be obvious insofar as people tend to practice religion in communities and there is a lot of evidence that it strengthens social bonds.[10] But spirituality itself appears to potentially lower loneliness as well. Scholars in 2019 asked 319 people to evaluate statements such as "I have a personally meaningful relationship with God." They found a strong negative correlation between spiritual affirmations and loneliness, leading to higher levels of mental health.[11]

Here's the bottom line: spiritual, religious, and other metaphysical experiences are not an imaginary phenomenon. They affect your brain, and give you access to insights and knowledge you can't get in other ways.

But doing so is filled with challenges. The three most common are our difficulty focusing, finding our path, and holding the right motives. These are the challenges we take on in this chapter.

Challenge 1

YOUR MONKEY MIND

One of the biggest problems with a life is that, well, we miss too much of it. Not literally, of course, but think about it: How much of your time are you really present? We are not completely conscious of the present moment most of the time in ordinary life. Much of our attention is on the past and future—at the expense of being mindfully in the here and now. If you don't believe it, just observe your thoughts at any moment, jumping around like a crazy monkey. One minute you are ruminating on what somebody told you last week; the next you are thinking about what you plan to do on the weekend. In the meantime, you are missing your life right now.

Now, close your eyes in meditation or prayer. You become truly present in this moment of your life—you are mindful. In other words, the transcendent gives you more of your life to experience.

Yet we don't do it very much. Humans have a

remarkable ability to resist living in the present moment. Indeed, the quintessential humanness of the mind is the ability to rerun past events and pre-run future scenarios. This is a great blessing, of course, as it allows us to learn maximally from our experiences and effectively practice for the future. It is also a curse. The Vietnamese Buddhist monk Thích Nhất Hạnh explained this in his book **The Miracle of Mindfulness:** "While washing the dishes, one should only be washing the dishes, which means that while washing the dishes one should be completely aware of the fact that one is washing the dishes."[12] If we are thinking about the past or future, "we are not alive during the time we are washing the dishes."

You don't have to be a follower of Buddhism to know that mindfulness is all the rage. Across dozens of apps and websites, you can learn the latest techniques. Besides putting you in the here and now, research finds that it may be a remedy for many personal problems. It has been shown to lessen depression, lower anxiety, improve memory, and decrease back pain.[13] It can even raise test scores.[14]

If mindfulness is so great, then why aren't all of us practicing it every day? Why are we still spending so much time romanticizing or regretting the past and anticipating the future? The answer is that mindfulness is not natural, and it's actually quite hard. Many psychologists believe that as a species, humans are not evolved to enjoy the here and now. Rather, we are wired to think about the past and especially the future, to consider new scenarios and try out new ideas. The psychologist Martin Seligman goes so far as to call our species **Homo prospectus,** meaning we naturally reside in the future.[15]

Avoiding mindfulness can also be an effective way to distract yourself from pain. Researchers have shown that people's minds are significantly more likely to wander when they're in a negative mood than when they're in a positive mood.[16] Some sources of unhappiness that lead to distraction and mind-wandering are fear, anxiety, neuroticism, and, of course, boredom.[17] Having a negative self-perception—feeling ashamed of yourself, for example—is also likely to lead to distraction from the here and now. Scholars have shown that people who suffered from a lot of shame tended to mind-wander considerably more than those who did not.[18]

If you struggle with mindfulness, two underlying problems might be to blame: you don't know how to be at home in your head, or you **do** know and have concluded that home is no fun. If the former is what's stopping you, then by all means, dig into the extensive and growing technology and literature on mindfulness. You might try formal meditation or simply paying attention more to your current surroundings.

If your problem is the latter, you need to face the source of fear and discomfort head-on. Avoiding yourself won't work in the long run; in fact, a lot of research shows that mind-wandering to avoid emotions makes things worse, not better.[19] You might choose to take on the source of your unhappiness in the here and now with professional assistance, just as you might seek help from a counselor about a marital problem. But even just acknowledging your uncomfortable emotions—your fear, shame, guilt, sadness, or anger—can be the beginning of the solution, insofar as it encourages you to confront your resistance to experiencing these feelings. It might be less unpleasant than you think.

Note that mindfulness is not the same thing as navel-gazing. To be here now does not mean obsessing over yourself and your problems and disregarding others. Scholars have shown that excessive self-concern can increase defensiveness and negativity.[20] Mindfulness should work instead toward a sense of yourself as part of the wider world, and an observation of your emotions without judgment. As you work to focus on the present, remind yourself of two things: you are just one of eight billion human beings; and your emotions will come and go as a normal part of being alive. The tools of metacognition discussed earlier in this book should be a big help to you as you work to become more mindful.

There will still be times when you will be distracted—you're only human, after all. And at times, you might even want to do so purposively. For example, you might choose to read a magazine while waiting at the dentist to avoid thinking about your impending root canal. The key here is that you are making an occasional choice, meaning that you are in fact managing your emotions, rather than allowing them to manage you. In this case, distraction is one tool in your emotional arsenal to be used sparingly—but mindfulness should always be your default.

Challenge 2

GETTING STARTED

The most important part of starting (or supercharging) a transcendental journey is, well, **starting.** People go their whole lives **wishing** they had faith, but not doing the work. Enlightenment doesn't just come, like a change in the weather. It requires serious attention. And like anything else—going to college, getting in better physical shape—the hardest part is just starting, which is a choice.

Here are a few ideas to help.

First, keep it simple. Good professional fitness trainers who specialize in clients who haven't exercised in many years (or perhaps ever) never start with a complicated battery of tests and a step-by-step protocol of exercises. For the first few weeks, the client is encouraged to do something easy and active for one hour a day. Usually, that means going for a walk. (More on that in a moment.) Similarly, when people ask how to get started on a spiritual path, the best answer is not beginning with a thirty-day silent retreat in the Himalayas, sitting in the lotus position—the equivalent of trying to deadlift your body weight on your first visit to the gym. Rather, it is something easy and simple—like slipping into a religious service and sitting in the back, observing without judgment or expectation.

Second, read more. A transcendental practice requires learning. Start reading widely from the wisdom literatures, including your own tradition, if you have one. In a similar spirit as our last piece of advice, don't start with the densest texts. Rather than trying to get through the Buddha's discourses in the original Pali or Thomas Aquinas's **Summa Theologiae,** try a more popular title on Buddhism or Christianity at your library or bookstore.[21]

Third, let go. You are committed to managing your own life. You are willing to do the work to get happier, which is great. But this tendency might come at a cost. Specifically, you might tend to want to control things. A need to control everything can be an impediment in your spiritual journey, which often requires an intuitive attitude—to allow yourself, in a childlike way, to have experiences you don't understand, as opposed to strangling them with facts and knowledge. There is irony in mentioning this in a book about the science of happiness, of course. But scholars have shown that people who have a more intuitive reasoning style—who answer questions based on "feel"—reported stronger religious beliefs than those who were more analytical.[22] This finding was independent of differences in education, income, political views, and intelligence. In other words, don't rule something out just because you can't explain it.

Maybe you have read this far and are throwing up your hands, saying, "I don't get it. I'm just not a spiritual person." OK, fine. Then just do one thing: go outside and connect with the outdoors. This is one of the most time-tested ways to have a transcendental experience.

Unfortunately, it is increasingly rare. After all, the percentage of Americans working outdoors fell from 90 percent at the beginning of the nineteenth century to less than 20 percent at the close of the twentieth century.[23] We show the same pattern in our pursuit of leisure: Americans went on one billion fewer outings in nature in 2018 compared with 2008.[24] Today, 85 percent of adults say they spent more time outside when they were kids than children do today.[25] The trend away from nature over the past few centuries, and especially the past few decades, has straightforward explanations. To begin with, the world's population has urbanized, so nature is less at hand. According to US census data, 6.1 percent of the American population resided in urban areas in 1800; in 2000, 79 percent did.[26] Second, no matter where you live, technology is displacing the outdoors in your attention. A 2017 study noted that screen time is rising rapidly for all age groups—adults averaged 10 hours and 39 minutes a day in 2016—even as hunting, fishing, camping, and children's outdoor play have declined substantially.[27]

Perhaps you are an urbanite with an indoor job, tied to your devices all day and night—and besides walking from your house to the car or train, you haven't spent serious time in nature in months or even years. If so, you are probably suffering some noticeable malaise, such as stress, anxiety, or even depression. In one study from 2015, researchers assigned people to walk in either nature or an urban setting for fifty minutes.[28] The nature walkers had lower anxiety, better mood, and better working memory. They were also much less likely to agree with statements such as "I often reflect on episodes of my life that I should no longer concern myself with."

A focus on the metaphysical makes you a lot less concerned with the opinions of others. It's no surprise that exposure to nature does the same thing. In 2008, researchers found that people who walked in a city for fifteen minutes were 39 percent more likely to agree with the statement "Right now, I am concerned about the way I present myself" than people who spent the same amount of time walking in nature.[29]

If you still need convincing, maybe a few words from the American writer Henry David Thoreau—who believed in the transcendental power of nature—

will help. "I was walking in a meadow, the source of a small brook, when the sun at last, just before setting, after a cold, gray day, reached a clear stratum in the horizon," he wrote in 1862.[30] In this ordinary experience, he found the sublime, as if he were walking to the Holy Land—"till one day the sun shall shine more brightly than ever he has done, shall perchance shine into our minds and hearts, and light up our whole lives with a great awakening light, as warm and serene and golden as on a bankside in autumn."

Thoreau believed that nature has powers beyond our understanding—that contact with the earth transforms us. Modern science says he was probably right.[31] Researchers have found that exposure to natural light (but not artificial light) synchronizes your internal circadian clock to the rising and setting of the sun.[32] (Ditch your devices and even artificial lights for a few days and sleeping naturally might be easier than ever.) Similarly, some small experiments have found that when people are in physical contact with the earth in ways as simple as walking barefoot outdoors—known as "earthing" or "grounding" the human body—their self-reported health and mood can improve. If you want to feel better, take your shoes off and spend the day outside; it might help.[33]

Here's the bottom line: There are any number of ways to get started on a transcendental journey. It doesn't have to be complicated or esoteric; in fact, it should start modestly and simply. Pray a little, read a little, let go, go for a walk outside without devices. The important thing is to start.

Challenge 3

THE RIGHT FOCUS

The biggest mistake people make when seeking a spiritual path is pursuing it for their personal ends. The earlier chapters on family and friendship pointed out a paradox: we tend to get love most when we give it freely. Faith and spirituality feature a similar paradox. Namely, you get the personal benefit primarily when that benefit is **not** the goal.

A Tibetan Buddhist monk once made this point when he gently chided many American practitioners of Buddhism.[34] "So many American Buddhists practice in order to relieve their personal problems," he said. "They do not understand that the true point is to seek the truth and relieve others of their suffering." To be more specific, in Buddhism, the goal of the practitioner is to be a bodhisattva—to achieve a Buddha nature and thus break out of the endless cycle of suffering in birth and death, yet choose not to do so, so as to remain in this cycle of life to help others achieve greater enlightenment as well.

The Japanese Zen Buddhists teach their faith using koans, or riddles to meditate on. One of the most famous is "What is the sound of one hand clapping?" It seems like a nonsensical question until you realize the answer: "An illusion." One hand in a clapping movement can make you imagine a clapping sound, but it does not make a real sound until a second hand is added. This illustrates the Buddhist idea of emptiness—that each of us is empty of meaning until we are in communion with others. To enjoy love, you must love others and be loved by them. That is why a bodhisattva meditates—not to relieve his own stress and anxiety, but to focus on the stress and anxiety of others.

This is the mystical truth behind almost all faiths and traditions. Serve the tenets of the divine, seek the ultimate truth, and thus work to make others happier rather than yourself. Only **then** will you be more successful in your own quest.

This paradox is summed up by C. S. Lewis in his famous book **Mere Christianity,** in his description of a man named Dick who wants to be happy and good. "As long as Dick does not turn to God, he thinks his niceness is his own, and just as long as he thinks that, it is not his own. It is only when Dick realizes that his niceness is not his own but a gift from God, and when he offers it back to God—it is just then that it begins to be really his own. For now Dick is beginning to take a share in his own creation. The only things we can keep are the things we freely give to God. What we try to keep for ourselves is just what we are sure to lose."[35]

If you walk the transcendental path, you will

get happier, but only if getting happier is not your goal. Your goal must be seeking truth and the good of others.

THE WAY FORWARD

We can't tell you what your transcendental path should be, but we can tell you that you will build a better life if you pursue one. The science clearly shows that metaphysical experiences are not superstitious nonsense, but rather provide a benefit to your happiness you cannot get elsewhere. Finding and following your path presents challenges, of course, of which we have laid out three of the biggest. Take on the following lessons using your management skills, and you will experience the greatest gain.

1. Spiritual life can be hard because it goes against the stimuli around us that constantly fragment our attention. We must work to be present and mindful, and we can get better at doing so.
2. It is an error to wait around and hope that a spiritual practice finds us; that probably won't occur. We need to do the work to build a spiritual practice, just like anything else of value. The most important step is the first one.
3. The focus of a faith or spiritual practice must not be primarily an inner one. The benefit to

> ourselves is immense, but the motive must be a search for truth and the love of others.

Unlike the lessons in the preceding chapters, these are harder to put into immediate practice, with immediate results. So let's add a fourth lesson, to usher in the first three over the coming months and years of your life: Commit a set period of time each day to your spiritual or philosophical life. For example, start your morning with just fifteen minutes of reading wisdom literature and sitting in contemplation or prayer. If your house is too crazy for that, find that slot during your lunch break or in the evening. At first, fifteen minutes will feel like a lot, but it will get easier over time, and if you keep at it, you will want to extend it. The key to success at the beginning, though, is consistency. Just fifteen minutes, every day.

This brings us to the end of the second phase in the plan to build the life you want. Pay attention and manage what matters—the four fundamental pillars of family, friendship, work, and faith—by taking on the greatest challenges to each one.

In these eight chapters, we have covered an enormous amount of knowledge, spanning literally thousands of scientific studies. No doubt many of the lessons and concepts surprised you. Many others you knew, but you needed to be reminded. But probably all of them made basic sense. In general, happiness lessons should always pass the "Grandma test." (If Grandma would say, "That's nonsense," you should be **very** suspicious.)

The challenge now is remembering the lessons. For most people, life's complications make it easy to forget new ideas and slip back into old patterns. For this reason, this book finishes with a truly surefire way to cement the principles of building your life and getting happier: become the teacher.

A Note from Oprah

I have loved learning ever since I was a little girl. I have also loved sharing what I've learned. In fact, as I write this it seems to me that knowledge is never really complete **until** it's shared.

For me, **The Oprah Winfrey Show** was always at heart a classroom. I was curious about so many things, from the intricacies of the digestive system to the meaning of life. There was so much I wanted to know, so many questions to be asked and answered—and I figured other people were likewise curious and questioning, so I invited guests to come and be our teachers. Of course, it turned out that many members of the audience also had wisdom to share. So many people came to the show and shared so much.

The joy of shared knowledge also explains why I started a book club. The novels and memoirs that mean the most to me are the ones that open my eyes to deeper truths and new experiences, or bring meaningful ideas into sharper focus—and it's not in my nature to keep these truths and experiences and ideas to myself! Even as I'm reading a book I love, I'm imagining talking about it with other people, and that only enhances my enjoyment.

The truth is, I have always felt called to be a teacher, and I say that with no hubris in my heart. In my view, a teacher is not the one who knows everything; it's simply the one who shares what they've learned.

I have taught classes and workshops at my girls' school in South Africa, but mostly my role there is mentor. (Well, mentor and student. I could write a book about the tough lessons I learned in the process of building a school. Not to mention the lessons the girls themselves continually teach me. The sheer number of them—hundreds by now—reinforces the lesson of detached attachment I mentioned earlier. It's just not possible to be invested in specific outcomes for so many girls, each of whom has her own background, her own abilities, her own dreams and desires. My job is to open the door for them; only they can decide what they'll do when they walk through.)

When I'm mentoring "my girls," I like to emphasize that success in life isn't as much about having the right answers as it is about asking the good questions: What does living well mean—for me, not according to someone else's model—and how do I do it? What is genuinely worth striving for? What can I offer, and how can I serve? What lessons can I glean from my experiences, especially the toughest ones? How do I make the best use of my limited time on this earth?

It's no coincidence that these are the very same questions Arthur Brooks has explored in this book. They get to the heart of what it means to get happier. They acknowledge that it is an active process, a matter not of being but of becoming. And they spotlight the most important part of the process: your agency. They recognize that the person in control of your happiness—your **happierness**—is and forever will be you.

I see myself in so much of this book. And I suspect you have seen yourself, too. Not just the person you've been, but the truly happier person you can become. As I follow the principles that Arthur presents, **I** am becoming happier. I'm actually having fun—a word that previously didn't exist in my vocabulary because I was so work-focused. Now I'm traveling, adventuring, saying yes to new experiences—because I want to and not because I feel obligated. And I've verified many times over that happiness multiplies when we share it. I hope this book lets your sharing begin.

When you learn, teach.
When you get, give.
—Maya Angelou

Conclusion

Now, Become the Teacher

You picked up this book to build a happier life, and you've read a lot of ideas on how to do it. To put the ideas into practice, you have to remember them. Here's how to do that: teach what you've learned to a plastic platypus.

OK, you probably need some explanation here. There is a technique known as "plastic platypus learning," in which people are instructed to explain something they have learned to any inanimate object, such as, well . . . a plastic platypus. It could also be a rubber ducky or a bowling ball—that isn't the point. What the research on this technique shows is that if you can explain something coherently, you will absorb the information and remember it. The reason is pretty simple, and you already know it. You need to be **metacognitive** with the information—to use your prefrontal cortex—so you can understand and use it. And the best way to do that is to explain it clearly.

Even better than a plastic platypus, though, is a real person, and there has been a lot of research showing that teaching a subject is the most reliable way to learn it deeply. This was first demonstrated by the famous language teacher Jean-Pol Martin, who successfully taught foreign languages by making his students instruct one another.[1] Later research illustrated this concept in experiments in which one group of students studied materials by themselves while a second group explained them to others.[2] (They both had the same amount of time.) The second group (the student teachers) understood and remembered the material better than the first.

Teaching others how to get happier is about more than just solidifying the ideas in your own mind. With happiness in decline almost everywhere, and especially in the United States, our world needs advocates and warriors to help the millions suffering without relief. So many still believe that there is not hope as long as there is pain in their lives. Find the people in your life in this situation. Be their hope.

Now, you might be saying, "How can I help someone else build her life when mine is still a work in progress?" That is **precisely** when and why you are the most effective teacher. The best happiness teachers are the ones who have had to work to gain the knowledge they offer, not the lucky ones who fall out of bed every day in a great mood. Those lucky few are like the fitness influencers on Instagram who have superior genetics, eat whatever they want, and have no idea what the challenges are for the rest of us.

Don't hide your own struggles. Use them to help others understand that they are not alone, and getting happier is possible. Your pain gives you credibility, and your progress makes you an inspiration. And sharing with others increases that progress, making it the perfect win-win.

OLDER, WISER, HAPPIER

Teaching happiness is also the best strategy for getting happier as time goes on. One of the biggest sources of suffering for many people in middle age is the perception that while they have many years of life ahead, they are somehow declining in their abilities. This is especially true for people who have invested a lot in their skills.

If you feel like you have lost your edge or are a little burned out in middle age or beyond, this is normal. Researchers have long noted that many skills—analysis and innovation, for example—tend to rise quickly very early in life and then fall through one's thirties and forties. This is called fluid intelligence. It's what makes you good at what you do as a young adult, and you really notice it when it declines, which is usually earlier than you expect.[3]

There's another kind of intelligence that comes later, called crystallized intelligence, which is an increasing knack for combining complex ideas, understanding what they mean, recognizing patterns, and teaching others. This rises throughout middle age and can stay high well into old age. If you are over fifty and notice that you are better at seeing patterns and explaining ideas to others than you used to be, it's because your crystallized intelligence is higher.

The research on fluid and crystallized intelligence suggests that people should hold different roles throughout their lives that complement each type of smarts—but always tending toward teaching and mentoring others as the years pass, because that is your increasing natural strength. Maybe that is a change in job or career, or a different emphasis in what you do in your regular profession. The way we often see this play out for people who take time away from the workforce to raise their kids is that when the nest is empty, they return to work in a different kind of role than the one they left years earlier.

This isn't just professional advice, by the way. In life, we do best and are happiest when we rely more on our wisdom as we age. One of the reasons people love being grandparents so much—besides the fact that you can spoil the kids all day and then they go home!—is because it relies on crystallized intelligence. Grandparents lean on their experience and wisdom and tend not to freak out over little things, which makes everything easier and more fun.

And this brings us back to teaching the lessons for getting happier. As you age, becoming a happiness teacher will feel more and more natural to you. The older you get, the more this information will become truly yours. Others will seek you out to learn it.

THE MOST IMPORTANT BUILDING BLOCK OF ALL

As you've read this book, you may have noticed a running theme: every practice that helps you build the life you want is based on one thing.

Love.

To embark on a project to get happier, and to do the work to manage your emotions, is to say that you love yourself enough to make this investment. All of the pillars of happiness are about love, too: love for your family, love for your friends, love made visible by bringing your best self to work, and love for the divine through your transcendent journey. And to become the teacher of what you have learned is an act of abundant love toward everyone in your life.

Like happiness, love isn't a feeling. As Martin Luther King Jr., put it in 1957, "Love is not this sentimental something that we talk about. It's not merely an emotional something. Love is creative, understanding goodwill for all."[4] Love is a commitment, an act of will and discipline. Love, like getting happier, is something that you get better at with practice. It becomes more automatic with repetition. It becomes a habit over time. And when it does, everything else falls into place.

Start each day saying, "I don't know what this day will bring, but I will love others and allow myself to be loved." Whenever you are wondering what to do in a particular situation—whether it's big, like deciding to take a new job, or little, like letting someone into your lane in traffic—ask, "What is the most loving thing to do right now?" Armed with the knowledge you have gained in this book, you will never go wrong.

Of course, you aren't made of stone, and even if you commit to emotional self-management and to building your family, friendships, work, and faith, you will still have days when love seems out of reach. You will react badly to someone; you will let your feelings get the better of you; you will throw up your hands in frustration. That's only natural. The key to progress isn't perfection, it's to begin again, and again, and again. Every day is a new day, and another opportunity to pick up the hammer and go back to work. Just remind yourself that the life you want is built on love, and start again.

The two of us are doing the same with our own

lives. We are part of the same project—to get happier by building our lives on a foundation of love. This is the principle that brought us together in this partnership, and to write this book.

So just remember, we are walking alongside you, wishing you our very best in your journey. And we ask that you do the same for us. Strengthening one another, we can help each other build the lives we want. And together, we can maybe even help build the world we want as well.

For more information on building the life you want and teaching others to do the same, visit www.arthurbrooks.com/build.

Acknowledgments

We loved working together on this book. However, we didn't just hole up at Oprah's house and pound out the manuscript by ourselves. Many others made it possible with their ideas, hard work, and support.

We are grateful to our research team of Rena Rudavsky, Reece Brown, and Bryce Fuemmeler, who chased down thousands of references and checked fact after fact. Professor Joshua Greene at Harvard vetted the neuroscience in this book, and gave us feedback that improved the manuscript. Oprah thanks Deborah Way for helping her corral the words and language to speak of happiness. Meanwhile, Tara Montgomery, Candice Gayl, and Bob Greene gave us critical input and kept the book on track through a chaotic schedule. Nicole Nichols, Chelsea Hettrick, and Nicole Marostica ran communications, making sure the world knows about the project. And nothing would get done were it not for the support of many colleagues at Harpo and ACB Ideas, especially Rachel Ayerst Manfredi, Molly Glaeser, Olivia Ladner, Joanna Moss, Samantha Ray, and Mary Riner.

For their encouragement and guidance throughout, we're indebted to Bria Sandford, our editor at Portfolio; Anthony Mattero, Arthur's literary agent at Creative Artists Agency; and our legal representatives Marc Chamlin and Ken Weinrib.

Arthur thanks the leadership and his colleagues at the Harvard Kennedy School and Harvard Business School for creating a supportive and creative academic home where this work can flourish. The MBA students in his Leadership and Happiness classes at HBS, and the participants and supporters of the Leadership and Happiness Laboratory at HKS, are an inspiring reminder that happiness is something we can improve and share. Arthur is also indebted to **The Atlantic,** where many of the ideas and some of the passages in this book originally appeared in Arthur's weekly How to Build a Life column. Special thanks to Jeff Goldberg, Rachel Gutman-Wei, Julie Beck, and Ena Alvarado-Esteller, who make the column possible each week. Arthur's research is generously supported by Dan D'Aniello, Ravenel Curry, Tully Friedman, Cindy and Chris Galvin, and Eric Schmidt.

As we make clear in this book, happiness is built at home, in the bonds we count on in good times and bad. We would be in no shape to advise anyone on getting happier were it not for the love and support of our families. For Arthur, this starts with Ester Munt-Brooks, Arthur's wife and spiritual guru; also Joaquim, Carlos, Marina, Jessica, and Caitlin Brooks. For Oprah, thanks to all my Dear Ones, you know who you are, who make me happier every day.

Notes

Introduction: Albina's Secret

In the real-life stories in this introduction, except where indicated, fictional names are used and some details have been changed to protect the anonymity of the people quoted.

1. Michael Davern, Rene Bautista, Jeremy Freese, Stephen L. Morgan, and Tom W. Smith, General Social Surveys, 1972–2021 Cross-section, NORC, University of Chicago, gssdataexplorer.norc.org.
2. Renee D. Goodwin, Lisa C. Dierker, Melody Wu, Sandro Galea, Christina W. Hoven, and Andrea H. Weinberger, "Trends in US Depression Prevalence from 2015 to 2020: The Widening Treatment Gap," **American Journal of Preventive Medicine** 63, no. 5 (2022): 726–33.
3. Davern et al., General Social Surveys, 1972–2021 Cross-section.
4. **Global Happiness Study: What Makes People**

Happy around the World, Ipsos Global Advisor, August 2019.

Chapter One: Happiness Is Not the Goal, and Unhappiness Is Not the Enemy

This chapter adapts ideas and takes passages from the following essays:

Arthur C. Brooks, "Sit with Negative Emotions, Don't Push Them Away," How to Build a Life, **The Atlantic,** June 18, 2020; Arthur C. Brooks, "Measuring Your Happiness Can Help Improve It," How to Build a Life, **The Atlantic,** December 3, 2020; Arthur C. Brooks, "There Are Two Kinds of Happy People," How to Build a Life, **The Atlantic,** January 28, 2021; Arthur C. Brooks, "Different Cultures Define Happiness Differently," How to Build a Life, **The Atlantic,** July 15, 2021; Arthur C. Brooks, "The Meaning of Life Is Surprisingly Simple," How to Build a Life, **The Atlantic,** October 21, 2021; Arthur C. Brooks, "The Problem with 'No Regrets,'" How to Build a Life, **The Atlantic,** February 3, 2022; Arthur C. Brooks, "How to Want Less," How to Build a Life, **The Atlantic,** February 8, 2022; Arthur C. Brooks, "Choose Enjoyment over Pleasure," How to Build a Life, **The Atlantic,** March 24, 2022; Arthur C. Brooks, "What the Second-Happiest People Get Right," How to Build a Life, **The Atlantic,** March 31, 2022; Arthur C. Brooks, "How to Stop Freaking Out," How to Build a Life, **The Atlantic,** April 28, 2022; Arthur C. Brooks, "A Happiness Columnist's Three

Biggest Happiness Rules," How to Build a Life, **The Atlantic,** July 21, 2022; Arthur C. Brooks, "America Is Pursuing Happiness in All the Wrong Places," **The Atlantic,** November 16, 2022.

1. Jeffrey Zaslow, "A Beloved Professor Delivers the Lecture of a Lifetime," **Wall Street Journal,** September 20, 2007.
2. Saint Augustine, **The City of God,** book XI, ed. and trans. Marcus Dods (Edinburgh: T. & T. Clark, 1871), chapter 26, published online by Project Gutenberg.
3. E. E. Hewitt, "Sunshine in the Soul," Hymnary .org.
4. Yukiko Uchida and Yuji Ogihara, "Personal or Interpersonal Construal of Happiness: A Cultural Psychological Perspective," **International Journal of Wellbeing** 2, no. 4 (2012): 354–369.
5. Shigehiro Oishi, Jesse Graham, Selin Kesebir, and Iolanda Costa Galinha, "Concepts of Happiness across Time and Cultures," **Personality and Social Psychology Bulletin** 39, no. 5 (2013): 559–77.
6. Dictionary.com, s.v. "happiness," www.dictionary .com/browse/happiness.
7. Anna J. Clark, **Divine Qualities: Cult and Community in Republican Rome** (Oxford, UK: Oxford University Press, 2007).
8. Anna Altman, "The Year of Hygge, the Danish Obsession with Getting Cozy," **New Yorker,** December 18, 2016.
9. Philip Brickman and Donald T. Campbell, "Hedonic

Relativism and Planning the Good Society," in **Adaptation Level Theory,** ed. M. H. Appley (New York: Academic Press, 1971): 287–301.

10. Viktor E. Frankl, **Man's Search for Meaning** (Boston: Beacon Press, 1946), xvii.
11. Catherine J. Norris, Jackie Gollan, Gary G. Berntson, and John T. Cacioppo, "The Current Status of Research on the Structure of Evaluative Space," **Biological Psychology** 84, no. 3 (2010): 422–36.
12. Jordi Quoidbach, June Gruber, Moïra Mikolajczak, Alexsandr Kogan, Ilios Kotsou, and Michael I. Norton, "Emodiversity and the Emotional Ecosystem," **Journal of Experimental Psychology: General** 143, no. 6 (2014): 2057–66.
13. Richard J. Davidson, Alexander J. Shackman, and Jeffrey S. Maxwell, "Asymmetries in Face and Brain Related to Emotion," **Trends in Cognitive Sciences** 8, no. 9 (2004): 389–91.
14. Debra Trampe, Jordi Quoidbach, and Maxime Taquet, "Emotions in Everyday Life," **PLoS One** 10, no. 12 (2015): e0145450.
15. Daniel Kahneman, Alan B. Krueger, David A. Schkade, Norbert Schwarz, and Arthur A. Stone, "A Survey Method for Characterizing Daily Life Experience: The Day Reconstruction Method," **Science** 306, no. 5702 (2004): 1776–80.
16. David Watson, Lee Anna Clark, and Auke Tellegen, "Development and Validation of Brief Measures of Positive and Negative Affect: The PANAS Scales," **Journal of Personality and Social Psychology** 54, no. 6 (1988): 1063–70. Readers can take this test by

going to www.authentichappiness.sas.upenn.edu/testcenter.

17. The averages are taken from the original research of Watson, Clark, and Tellegen (1988).
18. Kristen A. Lindquist, Ajay B. Satpute, Tor D. Wager, Jochen Weber, and Lisa Feldman Barrett, "The Brain Basis of Positive and Negative Affect: Evidence from a Meta-analysis of the Human Neuroimaging Literature," **Cerebral Cortex** 26, no. 5 (2016): 1910–22.
19. Paul Rozin and Edward B. Royzman, "Negativity Bias, Negativity Dominance, and Contagion," **Personality and Social Psychology Review** 5, no. 4 (2001): 296–320.
20. Emmy Gut, "Productive and Unproductive Depression: Interference in the Adaptive Function of the Basic Depressed Response," **British Journal of Psychotherapy** 2, no. 2 (1985): 95–113.
21. Neal J. Roese, Kai Epstude, Florian Fessel, Mike Morrison, Rachel Smallman, Amy Summerville, Adam D. Galinsky, and Suzanne Segerstrom, "Repetitive Regret, Depression, and Anxiety: Findings from a Nationally Representative Survey," **Journal of Social and Clinical Psychology** 28, no. 6 (2009): 671–88.
22. Melanie Greenberg, "The Psychology of Regret: Should We Really Aim to Live Our Lives with No Regrets?" **Psychology Today,** May 16, 2012.
23. Daniel H. Pink, **The Power of Regret: How Looking Backward Moves Us Forward** (New York: Penguin, 2022). This quote came via email from the author.

24. John Keats, **The Letters of John Keats to His Family and Friends,** ed. Sidney Colvin (London: Macmillan and Co., 1925), published online by Project Gutenberg.
25. Karol Jan Borowiecki, "How Are You, My Dearest Mozart? Well-being and Creativity of Three Famous Composers Based on Their Letters," **Review of Economics and Statistics** 99, no. 4 (2017): 591–605.
26. Paul W. Andrews and J. Anderson Thomson Jr., "The Bright Side of Being Blue: Depression as an Adaptation for Analyzing Complex Problems," **Psychological Review** 116, no. 3 (2009): 620–54.
27. Shigehiro Oishi, Ed Diener, and Richard E. Lucas, "The Optimum Level of Well-being: Can People Be Too Happy?" in **The Science of Well-Being: The Collected Works of Ed Diener,** ed. Ed Diener (Heidelberg, London, and New York: Springer Dordrecht, 2009): 175–200.
28. June Gruber, Iris B. Mauss, and Maya Tamir, "A Dark Side of Happiness? How, When, and Why Happiness Is Not Always Good," **Perspectives on Psychological Science** 6, no. 3 (2011): 222–33.

Chapter Two: The Power of Metacognition

This chapter adapts ideas and takes passages from the following essays:

Arthur C. Brooks, "When You Can't Change the World, Change Your Feelings," How to Build a Life, **The Atlantic,** December 2, 2021; Arthur C. Brooks,

"How to Stop Freaking Out," How to Build a Life, **The Atlantic,** April 28, 2022; Arthur C. Brooks, "How to Make the Baggage of Your Past Easier to Carry," How to Build a Life, **The Atlantic,** June 16, 2022.

1. "Viktor Emil Frankl," Viktor Frankl Institut, www.viktorfrankl.org/biography.html.
2. Antonio Semerari, Antonino Carcione, Giancarlo Dimaggio, Maurizio Falcone, Giuseppe Nicolò, Michele Procacci, and Giorgio Alleva, "How to Evaluate Metacognitive Functioning in Psychotherapy? The Metacognition Assessment Scale and Its Applications," **Clinical Psychology & Psychotherapy** 10, no. 4 (2003): 238–61.
3. Paul D. MacLean, T. J. Boag, and D. Campbell, **A Triune Concept of the Brain and Behaviour: Hincks Memorial Lectures** (Toronto: University of Toronto Press, 1973).
4. Patrick R. Steffen, Dawson Hedges, and Rebekka Matheson, "The Brain Is Adaptive Not Triune: How the Brain Responds to Threat, Challenge, and Change," **Frontiers in Psychiatry** 13 (2022).
5. Trevor Huff, Navid Mahabadi, and Prasanna Tadi, "Neuroanatomy, Visual Cortex," StatPearls (2022).
6. Joseph LeDoux and Nathaniel D. Daw, "Surviving Threats: Neural Circuit and Computational Implications of a New Taxonomy of Defensive Behaviour," **Nature Reviews Neuroscience** 19, no. 5 (2018): 269–82; "Understanding the Stress Response," Harvard Health Publishing, July 6, 2020; Sean M. Smith and Wylie W. Vale, "The Role of the Hypothalamic-Pituitary-Adrenal Axis

in Neuroendocrine Responses to Stress," **Dialogues in Clinical Neuroscience** 8, no. 4 (2006): 383–95.

7. LeDoux and Daw, "Surviving Threats."
8. Carroll E. Izard, "Emotion Theory and Research: Highlights, Unanswered Questions, and Emerging Issues," **Annual Review of Psychology** 60 (2009): 1–25.
9. APA Dictionary of Psychology, s.v. "joy," American Psychological Association, accessed December 2, 2022, www.dictionary.apa.org/joy.
10. "From Thomas Jefferson to Thomas Jefferson Smith, 21 February 1825," Founders Online.
11. Jeffrey M. Osgood and Mark Muraven, "Does Counting to Ten Increase or Decrease Aggression? The Role of State Self-Control (Ego-Depletion) and Consequences," **Journal of Applied Social Psychology** 46, no. 2 (2016): 105–13.
12. Boethius, **The Consolation of Philosophy,** trans. H. R. James (London: Elliot Stock, 1897), published online by Project Gutenberg.
13. Amy Loughman, "Ancient Stress Response vs Modern Life," Mind Body Microbiome, January 9, 2020.
14. Jeremy Sutton, "Maladaptive Coping: 15 Examples & How to Break the Cycle," PositivePsychology.com, October 28, 2020.
15. Philip Phillips, "Boethius," Oxford Bibliographies, last modified March 30, 2017.
16. Boethius, **Consolation of Philosophy.**
17. Ralph Waldo Emerson, "Self-Reliance," in **Essays: First Series** (Boston: J. Munroe and Company, 1841).

18. Daniel L. Schacter, Donna Rose Addis, and Randy L. Buckner, "Remembering the Past to Imagine the Future: The Prospective Brain," **Nature Reviews Neuroscience** 8, no. 9 (2007): 657–61.
19. Marcus Raichle, "The Brain's Default Mode Network," **Annual Review of Neuroscience** 38 (2015): 433–47.
20. Ulric Neisser and Nicole Harsch, "Phantom Flashbulbs: False Recollections of Hearing the News about Challenger," in **Affect and Accuracy in Recall: Studies of "Flashbulb" Memories,** ed. E. Winograd and U. Neisser (Cambridge, UK: Cambridge University Press, 1992).
21. Melissa Fay Greene, "You Won't Remember the Pandemic the Way You Think You Will," **The Atlantic,** May 2021; Alisha C. Holland and Elizabeth A. Kensinger, "Emotion and Autobiographical Memory," **Physics of Life Reviews** 7, no. 1 (2010): 88–131.
22. Linda J. Levine and David A. Pizarro, "Emotion and Memory Research: A Grumpy Overview," **Social Cognition** 22, no. 5 (2004): 530–54.
23. "Maha-satipatthana Sutta: The Great Frames of Reference," trans. Thanissaro Bhikkhu, Access to Insight, 2000.
24. James W. Pennebaker, **Opening Up: The Healing Power of Expressing Emotions** (New York: Guilford Press, 2012).
25. Dorit Alt and Nirit Raichel, "Reflective Journaling and Metacognitive Awareness: Insights from a Longitudinal Study in Higher Education," **Reflective Practice** 21, no. 2 (2020): 145–58.

26. Seth J. Gillihan, Jennifer Kessler, and Martha J. Farah, "Memories Affect Mood: Evidence from Covert Experimental Assignment to Positive, Neutral, and Negative Memory Recall," **Acta Psychologica** 125, no. 2 (2007): 144–54.
27. Nic M. Westrate and Judith Glück, "Hard-Earned Wisdom: Exploratory Processing of Difficult Life Experience Is Positively Associated with Wisdom," **Developmental Psychology** 53, no. 4 (2017): 800–14.

Chapter Three: Choose a Better Emotion

This chapter adapts ideas and takes passages from the following essays:

Arthur C. Brooks, "Don't Wish for Happiness. Work for It," How to Build a Life, **The Atlantic,** April 22, 2021; Arthur C. Brooks, "The Link between Happiness and a Sense of Humor," How to Build a Life, **The Atlantic,** August 12, 2021; Arthur C. Brooks, "The Difference between Hope and Optimism," How to Build a Life, **The Atlantic,** September 23, 2021; Arthur C. Brooks, "How to Be Thankful When You Don't Feel Thankful," How to Build a Life, **The Atlantic,** November 24, 2021; Arthur C. Brooks, "How to Stop Dating People Who Are Wrong for You," How to Build a Life, **The Atlantic,** June 23, 2022.

1. Diane C. Mitchell, Carol A. Knight, Jon Hockenberry, Robyn Teplansky, and Terryl J. Hartman, "Beverage Caffeine Intakes in the

US," **Food and Chemical Toxicology** 63 (2014): 136–42.

2. Brian Fiani, Lawrence Zhu, Brian L. Musch, Sean Briceno, Ross Andel, Nasreen Sadeq, and Ali Z. Ansari, "The Neurophysiology of Caffeine as a Central Nervous System Stimulant and the Resultant Effects on Cognitive Function," **Cureus** 13, no. 5 (2021): e15032; Thomas V. Dunwiddie and Susan A. Masino, "The Role and Regulation of Adenosine in the Central Nervous System," **Annual Review of Neuroscience** 24, no. 1 (2001): 31–55; Leeana Aarthi Bagwath Persad, "Energy Drinks and the Neurophysiological Impact of Caffeine," **Frontiers in Neuroscience** 5 (2011): 116.
3. Paul Rozin and Edward B. Royzman, "Negativity Bias, Negativity Dominance, and Contagion," **Personality and Social Psychology Review** 5, no. 4 (2001): 296–320.
4. Charlotte vanOyen Witvliet, Fallon J. Richie, Lindsey M. Root Luna, and Daryl R. Van Tongeren, "Gratitude Predicts Hope and Happiness: A Two-Study Assessment of Traits and States," **Journal of Positive Psychology** 14, no. 3 (2019): 271–82.
5. Glenn R. Fox, Jonas Kaplan, Hanna Damasio, and Antonio Damasio, "Neural Correlates of Gratitude," **Frontiers in Psychology** 6 (2015): 1491; Kent C. Berridge and Morten L. Kringelbach, "Pleasure Systems in the Brain," **Neuron** 86, no. 3 (2015): 646–64.
6. Jane Taylor Wilson, "Brightening the Mind: The Impact of Practicing Gratitude on Focus and Resilience in Learning," **Journal of the Scholarship**

of Teaching and Learning 16, no. 4 (2016): 1–13; Nathaniel M. Lambert and Frank D. Fincham, "Expressing Gratitude to a Partner Leads to More Relationship Maintenance Behavior," **Emotion** 11, no. 1 (2011): 52–60; Sara B. Algoe, Barbara L. Fredrickson, and Shelly L. Gable, "The Social Functions of the Emotion of Gratitude Via Expression," **Emotion** 13, no. 4 (2013): 605–9; Maggie Stoeckel,
Carol Weissbrod, and Anthony Ahrens, "The Adolescent Response to Parental Illness: The Influence of Dispositional Gratitude," **Journal of Child and Family Studies** 24, no. 5 (2014): 1501–9.

7. Anna L. Boggiss, Nathan S. Consedine, Jennifer M. Brenton-Peters, Paul L. Hofman, and Anna S. Serlachius, "A Systematic Review of Gratitude Interventions: Effects on Physical Health and Health Behaviors," **Journal of Psychosomatic Research** 135 (2020): 110165; Megan M. Fritz, Christina N. Armenta, Lisa C. Walsh, and Sonja Lyubomirsky, "Gratitude Facilitates Healthy Eating Behavior in Adolescents and Young Adults," **Journal of Experimental Social Psychology** 81 (2019): 4–14.
8. M. Tullius Cicero, **The Orations of Marcus Tullius Cicero,** trans. C. D. Yonge (London: George Bell & Sons, 1891).
9. David DeSteno, Monica Y. Bartlett, Jolie Baumann, Lisa A. Williams, and Leah Dickens, "Gratitude as Moral Sentiment: Emotion-Guided Cooperation in Economic Exchange," **Emotion** 10, no. 2 (2010):

289–93; David DeSteno, Ye Li, Leah Dickens, and Jennifer S. Lerner, "Gratitude: A Tool for Reducing Economic Impatience," **Psychological Science** 25, no. 6 (2014): 1262–7; Jo-Ann Tsang, Thomas P. Carpenter, James A. Roberts, Michael B. Frisch, and Robert D. Carlisle, "Why Are Materialists Less Happy? The Role of Gratitude and Need Satisfaction in the Relationship between Materialism and Life Satisfaction," **Personality and Individual Differences** 64 (2014): 62–6.

10. Nathaniel M. Lambert, Frank D. Fincham, and Tyler F. Stillman, "Gratitude and Depressive Symptoms: The Role of Positive Reframing and Positive Emotion," **Cognition & Emotion** 26, no. 4 (2012): 615–33.
11. Kristin Layous and Sonja Lyubomirsky, "Benefits, Mechanisms, and New Directions for Teaching Gratitude to Children," **School Psychology Review** 43, no. 2 (2014): 153–9.
12. Nathaniel M. Lambert, Frank D. Fincham, Scott R. Braithwaite, Steven M. Graham, and Steven R. H. Beach, "Can Prayer Increase Gratitude?" **Psychology of Religion and Spirituality** 1, no. 3 (2009): 139–49.
13. Araceli Frias, Philip C. Watkins, Amy C. Webber, and Jeffrey J. Froh, "Death and Gratitude: Death Reflection Enhances Gratitude," **Journal of Positive Psychology** 6, no. 2 (2011): 154–62.
14. Ru H. Dai, Hsueh-Chih Chen, Yu C. Chan, Ching-Lin Wu, Ping Li, Shu L. Cho, and Jon-Fan Hu, "To Resolve or Not to Resolve, That Is the Question: The Dual-Path Model of Incongruity Resolution

and Absurd Verbal Humor by fMRI," **Frontiers in Psychology** 8 (2017): 498; Takeshi Satow, Keiko Usui, Masao Matsuhashi, J. Yamamoto, Tahamina Begum, Hiroshi Shibasaki, A. Ikeda, N. Mikuni, S. Miyamoto, and Naoya Hashimoto, "Mirth and Laughter Arising from Human Temporal Cortex," **Journal of Neurology, Neurosurgery & Psychiatry** 74, no. 7 (2003): 1004–5.

15. E. B. White and Katherine S. White, eds., **A Subtreasury of American Humor** (New York: Coward-McCann, 1941).
16. Mimi M. Y. Tse, Anna P. K. Lo, Tracy L. Y. Cheng, Eva K. K. Chan, Annie H. Y. Chan, and Helena S. W. Chung, "Humor Therapy: Relieving Chronic Pain and Enhancing Happiness for Older Adults," **Journal of Aging Research** 2010 (2010): 343574.
17. Kim R. Edwards and Rod A. Martin, "Humor Creation Ability and Mental Health: Are Funny People More Psychologically Healthy?" **Europe's Journal of Psychology** 6, no. 3 (2010): 196–212.
18. Victoria Ando, Gordon Claridge, and Ken Clark, "Psychotic Traits in Comedians," **British Journal of Psychiatry** 204, no. 5 (2014): 341–5.
19. Giovanni Boccaccio, **The Decameron of Giovanni Boccaccio,** trans. John Payne (New York: Walter J. Black), published online by Project Gutenberg.
20. John Morreall, "Religious Faith, Militarism, and Humorlessness," **Europe's Journal of Psychology** 1, no. 3 (2005).
21. Ori Amir and Irving Biederman, "The Neural Correlates of Humor Creativity," **Frontiers in**

Human Neuroscience 10 (2016): 597; Alan Feingold and Ronald Mazzella, "Psychometric Intelligence and Verbal Humor Ability," **Personality and Individual Differences** 12, no. 5 (1991): 427–35.

22. Edwards and Martin, "Humor Creation Ability."
23. David Hecht, "The Neural Basis of Optimism and Pessimism," **Experimental Neurobiology** 22, no. 3 (2013): 173–99.
24. Researchers have found that optimism may distort reality even more. Hecht, "Neural Basis of Optimism and Pessimism."
25. Jim Collins, **Good to Great: Why Some Companies Make the Leap . . . and Others Don't** (New York: HarperBusiness, 2001), 85.
26. Fred B. Bryant and Jamie A. Cvengros, "Distinguishing Hope and Optimism: Two Sides of a Coin, or Two Separate Coins?" **Journal of Social and Clinical Psychology** 23, no. 2 (2004): 273–302.
27. Anthony Scioli, Christine M. Chamberlin, Cindi M. Samor, Anne B. Lapointe, Tamara L. Campbell, Alex R. Macleod, and Jennifer McLenon, "A Prospective Study of Hope, Optimism, and Health," **Psychological Reports** 81, no. 3 (1997): 723–33.
28. Rebecca J. Reichard, James B. Avey, Shane Lopez, and Maren Dollwet, "Having the Will and Finding the Way: A Review and Meta-analysis of Hope at Work," **Journal of Positive Psychology** 8, no. 4 (2013): 292–304.
29. Liz Day, Katie Hanson, John Maltby, Carmel

Proctor, and Alex Wood, "Hope Uniquely Predicts Objective Academic Achievement above Intelligence, Personality, and Previous Academic Achievement," **Journal of Research in Personality** 44, no. 4 (2010): 550–3.

30. Stephen L. Stern, Rahul Dhanda, and Helen P. Hazuda, "Hopelessness Predicts Mortality in Older Mexican and European Americans," **Psychosomatic Medicine** 63, no. 3 (2001): 344–51.
31. Miriam A. Mosing, Brendan P. Zietsch, Sri N. Shekar, Margaret J. Wright, and Nicholas G. Martin, "Genetic and Environmental Influences on Optimism and Its Relationship to Mental and Self-Rated Health: A Study of Aging Twins," **Behavior Genetics** 39, no. 6 (2009): 597–604.
32. Dictionary.com, s.v. "empath," www.dictionary.com/browse/empath.
33. Psychiatric Medical Care Communications Team, "The Difference between Empathy and Sympathy," Psychiatric Medical Care.
34. Dana Brown, "The New Science of Empathy and Empaths (drjudithorloff.com)," **PACEsConnection** (blog), January 4, 2018; Ryszard Praszkier, "Empathy, Mirror Neurons and SYNC," **Mind & Society** 15, no. 1 (2016): 1–25.
35. Camille Fauchon, I. Faillenot, A. M. Perrin, C. Borg, Vincent Pichot, Florian Chouchou, Luis Garcia-Larrea, and Roland Peyron, "Does an Observer's Empathy Influence My Pain? Effect of Perceived Empathetic or Unempathetic Support on a Pain Test," **European Journal of Neuroscience** 46, no. 10 (2017): 2629–37.

36. Frans Derksen, Tim C. Olde Hartman, Annelies van Dijk, Annette Plouvier, Jozien Bensing, and Antoine Lagro-Janssen, "Consequences of the Presence and Absence of Empathy during Consultations in Primary Care: A Focus Group Study with Patients," **Patient Education and Counseling** 100, no. 5 (2017): 987–93.
37. Olga M. Klimecki, Susanne Leiberg, Matthieu Ricard, and Tania Singer, "Differential Pattern of Functional Brain Plasticity after Compassion and Empathy Training," **Social Cognitive and Affective Neuroscience** 9, no. 6 (2014): 873–9.
38. Paul Bloom, **Against Empathy: The Case for Rational Compassion** (New York: Random House, 2017), 2.
39. Clara Strauss, Billie Lever Taylor, Jenny Gu, Willem Kuyken, Ruth Baer, Fergal Jones, and Kate Cavanagh, "What Is Compassion and How Can We Measure It? A Review of Definitions and Measures," **Clinical Psychology Review** 47 (2016): 15–27.
40. Klimecki et al., "Differential Pattern."
41. Yawei Cheng, Ching-Po Lin, Ho-Ling Liu, Yuan-Yu Hsu, Kun-Eng Lim, Daisy Hung, and Jean Decety, "Expertise Modulates the Perception of Pain in Others," **Current Biology** 17, no. 19 (2007): 1708–13.
42. Varun Warrier, Roberto Toro, Bhismadev Chakrabarti, Anders D. Børglum, Jakob Grove, David A. Hinds, Thomas Bourgeron, and Simon Baron-Cohen, "Genome-Wide Analyses of Self-Reported Empathy: Correlations with

Autism, Schizophrenia, and Anorexia Nervosa," **Translational Psychiatry** 8, no. 1 (2018): 1–10; Aleksandr Kogan, Laura R. Saslow, Emily A. Impett, and Sarina Rodrigues Saturn, "Thin-Slicing Study of the Oxytocin Receptor (OXTR) Gene and the Evaluation and Expression of the Prosocial Disposition," **Proceedings of the National Academy of Sciences** 108, no. 48 (2011): 19189–92.

43. Hooria Jazaieri, Geshe Thupten Jinpa, Kelly McGonigal, Erika L. Rosenberg, Joel Finkelstein, Emiliana Simon-Thomas, Margaret Cullen, James R. Doty, James J. Gross, and Philippe R. Goldin, "Enhancing Compassion: A Randomized Controlled Trial of a Compassion Cultivation Training Program," **Journal of Happiness Studies** 14, no. 4 (2012): 1113–26.
44. Carrie Mok, Nirmal B. Shah, Stephen F. Goldberg, Amir C. Dayan, and Jaime L. Baratta, "Patient Perceptions and Expectations about Postoperative Analgesia" (presentation, Thomas Jefferson University Hospital, Philadelphia, 2018).

Chapter Four: Focus Less on Yourself

This chapter adapts ideas and takes passages from the following essays:

Arthur C. Brooks, "No One Cares," How to Build a Life, **The Atlantic,** November 11, 2021; Arthur C. Brooks, "Quit Lying to Yourself," How to Build a Life, **The Atlantic,** November 18, 2021; Arthur C. Brooks, "How to Stop Freaking Out," How to Build a Life, **The**

Atlantic, April 28, 2022; Arthur C. Brooks, "Don't Surround Yourself with Admirers," How to Build a Life, **The Atlantic,** June 30, 2022; Arthur C. Brooks, "Honesty Is Love," How to Build a Life, **The Atlantic,** August 18, 2022; Arthur C. Brooks, "A Shortcut for Feeling Just a Little Happier," How to Build a Life, **The Atlantic,** August 25, 2022; Arthur C. Brooks, "Envy, the Happiness Killer," How to Build a Life, **The Atlantic,** October 20, 2022.

1. Adam Waytz and Wilhelm Hofmann, "Nudging the Better Angels of Our Nature: A Field Experiment on Morality and Well-being," **Emotion** 20, no. 5 (2020): 904–9.
2. William James, **The Principles of Psychology** (New York: H. Holt and Company, 1890).
3. Michael Dambrun, "Self-Centeredness and Selflessness: Happiness Correlates and Mediating Psychological Processes," **PeerJ** 5 (2017): e3306.
4. Olga Khazan, "The Self-Confidence Tipping Point," **The Atlantic,** October 11, 2019; Leon F. Seltzer, "Self-Absorption: The Root of All (Psychological) Evil?" **Psychology Today,** August 24, 2016.
5. Marius Golubickis and C. Neil Macrae, "Sticky Me: Self-Relevance Slows Reinforcement Learning," **Cognition** 227 (2022): 105207.
6. Daisetz Teitaro Suzuki, **An Introduction to Zen Buddhism** (New York: Grove Press, 1991), 64.
7. This quote comes from email correspondence with one of the authors.
8. David Veale and Susan Riley, "Mirror, Mirror on the Wall, Who Is the Ugliest of Them All?

The Psychopathology of Mirror Gazing in Body Dysmorphic Disorder," **Behaviour Research and Therapy** 39, no. 12 (2001): 1381–93.

9. The man told Arthur this story.
10. Dacher Keltner, "Why Do We Feel Awe?" **Greater Good Magazine,** May 10, 2016.
11. Michelle N. Shiota, Dacher Keltner, and Amanda Mossman, "The Nature of Awe: Elicitors, Appraisals, and Effects on Self-Concept," **Cognition and Emotion** 21, no. 5 (2007): 944–63.
12. Wanshi Shôgaku, **Shôyôroku (Book of Equanimity): Introductions, Cases, Verses Selection of 100 Cases with Verses,** trans. Sanbô Kyôdan Society (2014).
13. Matthew 7:1, NIV.
14. Marcus Aurelius, **Meditations: A New Translation** (London: Random House UK, 2002), 162.
15. Richard Foley, **Intellectual Trust in Oneself and Others** (Cambridge, UK: Cambridge University Press, 2001).
16. Matthew D. Lieberman and Naomi I. Eisenberger, "The Dorsal Anterior Cingulate Cortex Is Selective for Pain: Results from Large-Scale Reverse Inference," **Proceedings of the National Academy of Sciences** 112, no. 49 (2015): 15250–5; Ruohe Zhao, Hang Zhou, Lianyan Huang, Zhongcong Xie, Jing Wang, Wen-Biao Gan, and Guang Yang, "Neuropathic Pain Causes Pyramidal Neuronal Hyperactivity in the Anterior Cingulate Cortex," **Frontiers in Cellular Neuroscience** 12 (2018): 107.
17. C. Nathan DeWall, Geoff MacDonald, Gregory D.

Webster, Carrie L. Masten, Roy F. Baumeister, Caitlin Powell, David Combs, David R. Schurtz, Tyler F. Stillman, Dianne M. Tice, Naomi I. Eisenberger, "Acetaminophen Reduces Social Pain: Behavioral and Neural Evidence," **Psychological Science** 21, no. 7 (2010): 931–7.

18. "Allodoxaphobia (a Complete Guide)," OptimistMinds, last modified February 3, 2023.
19. APA Dictionary of Psychology, s.v. "behavioral inhibition system," American Psychological Association, www.dictionary.apa.org/behavioral-inhibition-system; Marion R. M. Scholten et al., "Behavioral Inhibition System (BIS), Behavioral Activation System (BAS) and Schizophrenia: Relationship with Psychopathology and Physiology," **Journal of Psychiatric Research** 40, no. 7 (2006): 638–45.
20. Kees van den Bos, "Meaning Making Following Activation of the Behavioral Inhibition System: How Caring Less about What Others Think May Help Us to Make Sense of What Is Going On," in **The Psychology of Meaning,** ed. K. D. Markman, T. Proulx, and M. J. Lindberg (Washington, DC: American Psychological Association, 2013), 359–80.
21. Annette Kämmerer, "The Scientific Underpinnings and Impacts of Shame," **Scientific American,** August 9, 2019; Jay Boll, "Shame: The Other Emotion in Depression & Anxiety," Hope to Cope, March 8, 2021.
22. Lao Tzu, **Tao Te Ching: A New English Version,** trans. Stephen Mitchell (New York: Harper Perennial, 1992), poem 9.
23. No doubt you would love to stop caring what others

think; it gives you pain. But here's the problem: like regular pain, physical and emotional, it would be bad to erase it completely. That would be abnormal and dangerous; this tendency could lead to what psychologists call hubris syndrome or even be evidence of antisocial personality disorder. See David Owen and Jonathan Davidson, "Hubris Syndrome: An Acquired Personality Disorder? A Study of US Presidents and UK Prime Ministers over the Last 100 Years," **Brain** 132, no. 5 (2009): 1396–406; Robert J. Blair, "The Amygdala and Ventromedial Prefrontal Cortex in Morality and Psychopathy," **Trends in Cognitive Sciences** 11, no. 9 (2007): 387–92.

24. Kenneth Savitsky, Nicholas Epley, and Thomas Gilovich, "Do Others Judge Us as Harshly as We Think? Overestimating the Impact of Our Failures, Shortcomings, and Mishaps," **Journal of Personality and Social Psychology** 81, no. 1 (2001): 44–56.
25. Dante Alighieri, **The Divine Comedy,** trans. Henry Wadsworth Longfellow (Boston: 1867), published online by Project Gutenberg.
26. Joseph Epstein, **Envy: The Seven Deadly Sins,** vol. 1 (Oxford, UK: Oxford University Press, 2003), 1.
27. Jan Crusius, Manuel F. Gonzalez, Jens Lange, and Yochi Cohen-Charash, "Envy: An Adversarial Review and Comparison of Two Competing Views," **Emotion Review** 12, no. 1 (2020): 3–21.
28. Henrietta Bolló, Dzsenifer Roxána Háger, Manuel Galvan, and Gábor Orosz, "The Role of Subjective

and Objective Social Status in the Generation of Envy," **Frontiers in Psychology** 11 (2020): 513495.

29. Hidehiko Takahashi, Motoichiro Kato, Masato Matsuura, Dean Mobbs, Tetsuya Suhara, and Yoshiro Okubo, "When Your Gain Is My Pain and Your Pain Is My Gain: Neural Correlates of Envy and Schadenfreude," **Science** 323, no. 5916 (2009): 937–9.
30. Redzo Mujcic and Andrew J. Oswald, "Is Envy Harmful to a Society's Psychological Health and Wellbeing? A Longitudinal Study of 18,000 Adults," **Social Science & Medicine** 198 (2018): 103–11.
31. Nicole E. Henniger and Christine R. Harris, "Envy across Adulthood: The What and the Who," **Basic and Applied Social Psychology** 37, no. 6 (2015): 303–18.
32. Edson C. Tandoc Jr., Patrick Ferrucci, and Margaret Duffy, "Facebook Use, Envy, and Depression among College Students: Is Facebooking Depressing?" **Computers in Human Behavior** 43 (2015): 139–46.
33. Philippe Verduyn, David Seungjae Lee, Jiyoung Park, Holly Shablack, Ariana Orvell, Joseph Bayer, Oscar Ybarra, John Jonides, and Ethan Kross, "Passive Facebook Usage Undermines Affective Well-being: Experimental and Longitudinal Evidence," **Journal of Experimental Psychology: General** 144, no. 2 (2015): 480–8.
34. Cosimo de' Medici, Piero de' Medici, and Lorenzo de' Medici, **Lives of the Early Medici: As Told**

in Their Correspondence (Boston: R. G. Badger, 1911).

35. Ed O'Brien, Alexander C. Kristal, Phoebe C. Ellsworth, and Norbert Schwarz, "(Mis)imagining the Good Life and the Bad Life: Envy and Pity as a Function of the Focusing Illusion," **Journal of Experimental Social Psychology** 75 (2018): 41–53.
36. Alexandra Samuel, "What to Do When Social Media Inspires Envy," **JSTOR Daily,** February 6, 2018.
37. Alison Wood Brooks, Karen Huang, Nicole Abi-Esber, Ryan W. Buell, Laura Huang, and Brian Hall, "Mitigating Malicious Envy: Why Successful Individuals Should Reveal Their Failures," **Journal of Experimental Psychology: General** 148, no. 4 (2019): 667–87.
38. Ovul Sezer, Francesca Gino, and Michael I. Norton, "Humblebragging: A Distinct—and Ineffective—Self-Presentation Strategy," **Journal of Personality and Social Psychology** 114, no. 1 (2018): 52–74.

Chapter Five: Build Your Imperfect Family

This chapter adapts ideas and takes passages from the following essays:

Arthur C. Brooks, "Love Is Medicine for Fear," How to Build a Life, **The Atlantic,** July 16, 2020; Arthur C. Brooks, "There Are Two Kinds of Happy People," How to Build a Life, **The Atlantic,** January 28, 2021; Arthur C. Brooks, "Don't Wish for Happiness. Work for It," How to Build a Life, **The Atlantic,** April 22,

2021; Arthur C. Brooks, "How Adult Children Affect Their Mother's Happiness," How to Build a Life, **The Atlantic,** May 6, 2021; Arthur C. Brooks, "Dads Just Want to Help," How to Build a Life, **The Atlantic,** June 17, 2021; Arthur C. Brooks, "Those Who Share a Roof Share Emotions," How to Build a Life, **The Atlantic,** July 22, 2021; Arthur C. Brooks, "Fake Forgiveness Is Toxic for Relationships," How to Build a Life, **The Atlantic,** August 19, 2021; Arthur C. Brooks, "Quit Lying to Yourself," How to Build a Life, **The Atlantic,** November 18, 2021; Arthur C. Brooks, "The Common Dating Strategy That's Totally Wrong," How to Build a Life, **The Atlantic,** February 10, 2022; Arthur C. Brooks, "The Key to a Good Parent-Child Relationship? Low Expectations," How to Build a Life, **The Atlantic,** May 12, 2022; Arthur C. Brooks, "Honesty Is Love," How to Build a Life, **The Atlantic,** August 18, 2022.

1. Laura Silver, Patrick van Kessel, Christine Huang, Laura Clancy, and Sneha Gubbala, "What Makes Life Meaningful? Views from 17 Advanced Economies," Pew Research Center, November 18, 2021.
2. Christian Grevin, "The Chapman University Survey of American Fears, Wave 9" (Orange, CA: Earl Babbie Research Center, Chapman University, 2022).
3. Merril Silverstein and Roseann Giarrusso, "Aging and Family Life: A Decade Review," **Journal of Marriage and Family** 72, no. 5 (2010): 1039–58.
4. Leo Tolstoy, **Anna Karenina,** trans. Constance

Garnett (1901), published online by Project Gutenberg.

5. Adam Shapiro, "Revisiting the Generation Gap: Exploring the Relationships of Parent/Adult-Child Dyads," **International Journal of Aging and Human Development** 58, no. 2 (2004): 127–46.
6. Shapiro, "Revisiting the Generation Gap."
7. Joshua Coleman, "A Shift in American Family Values Is Fueling Estrangement," **The Atlantic,** January 10, 2021; Megan Gilligan, J. Jill Suitor, and Karl Pillemer, "Estrangement between Mothers and Adult Children: The Role of Norms and Values," **Journal of Marriage and Family** 77, no. 4 (2015): 908–20.
8. Kira S. Birditt, Laura M. Miller, Karen L. Fingerman, and Eva S. Lefkowitz, "Tensions in the Parent and Adult Child Relationship: Links to Solidarity and Ambivalence," **Psychology and Aging** 24, no. 2 (2009): 287–95.
9. Chris Segrin, Alesia Woszidlo, Michelle Givertz, Amy Bauer, and Melissa Taylor Murphy, "The Association between Overparenting, Parent-Child Communication, and Entitlement and Adaptive Traits in Adult Children," **Family Relations** 61, no. 2 (2012): 237–52.
10. Rhaina Cohen, "The Secret to a Fight-Free Relationship," **The Atlantic,** September 13, 2021.
11. Shapiro, "Revisiting the Generation Gap."
12. Kira S. Birditt, Karen L. Fingerman, Eva S. Lefkowitz, and Claire M. Kamp Dush, "Parents Perceived as Peers: Filial Maturity in Adulthood,"

Journal of Adult Development 15, no. 1 (2008): 1–12.

13. Ashley Fetters and Kaitlyn Tiffany, "The 'Dating Market' Is Getting Worse," **The Atlantic,** February 25, 2020.
14. Anna Brown, "Nearly Half of U.S. Adults Say Dating Has Gotten Harder for Most People in the Last 10 Years," Pew Research Center, August 20, 2020.
15. Michael Davern, Rene Bautista, Jeremy Freese, Stephen L. Morgan, and Tom W. Smith, General Social Surveys, 1972–2021 Cross-section, NORC, University of Chicago, gssdataexplorer.norc.org.
16. Christopher Ingraham, "The Share of Americans Not Having Sex Has Reached a Record High," **Washington Post,** March 29, 2019; Kate Julian, "Why Are Young People Having So Little Sex?" **The Atlantic,** December 15, 2018.
17. Gregory A. Huber and Neil Malhotra, "Political Homophily in Social Relationships: Evidence from Online Dating Behavior," **Journal of Politics** 79, no. 1 (2017): 269–83.
18. Cat Hofacker, "OkCupid: Millennials Say Personal Politics Can Make or Break a Relationship," **USA Today,** October 16, 2018.
19. Neal Rothschild, "Young Dems More Likely to Despise the Other Party," **Axios,** December 7, 2021.
20. "Is Education Doing Favors for Your Dating Life?" **GCU Experience** (blog), Grand Canyon University, June 22, 2021.
21. Robert F. Winch, "The Theory of Complementary

Needs in Mate-Selection: A Test of One Kind of Complementariness," **American Sociological Review** 20, no. 1 (1955): 52–6.

22. Pamela Sadler and Erik Woody, "Is Who You Are Who You're Talking To? Interpersonal Style and Complementarity in Mixed-Sex Interactions," **Journal of Personality and Social Psychology** 84, no. 1 (2003): 80–96.
23. Aurelio José Figueredo, Jon Adam Sefcek, and Daniel Nelson Jones, "The Ideal Romantic Partner Personality," **Personality and Individual Differences** 41, no. 3 (2006): 431–41.
24. Marc Spehr, Kevin R. Kelliher, Xiao-Hong Li, Thomas Boehm, Trese Leinders-Zufall, and Frank Zufall, "Essential Role of the Main Olfactory System in Social Recognition of Major Histocompatibility Complex Peptide Ligands," **Journal of Neuroscience** 26, no. 7 (2006): 1961–70.
25. Claus Wedekind, Thomas Seebeck, Florence Bettens, and Alexander J. Paepke, "MHC-Dependent Mate Preferences in Humans," **Proceedings of the Royal Society B: Biological Sciences** 260, no. 1359 (1995): 245–9.
26. Pablo Sandro Carvalho Santos, Juliano Augusto Schinemann, Juarez Gabardo, and Maria da Graça Bicalho, "New Evidence That the MHC Influences Odor Perception in Humans: A Study with 58 Southern Brazilian Students," **Hormones and Behavior** 47, no. 4 (2005): 384–8.
27. Michael J. Rosenfeld, Reuben J. Thomas, and Sonia Hausen, "Disintermediating Your Friends: How Online Dating in the United States Displaces

Other Ways of Meeting," **Proceedings of the National Academy of Sciences** 116, no. 36 (2019): 17753–8.

28. Jon Levy, Devin Markell, and Moran Cerf, "Polar Similars: Using Massive Mobile Dating Data to Predict Synchronization and Similarity in Dating Preferences," **Frontiers in Psychology** 10 (2019): 2010.
29. C. Price, "43% of Americans Have Gone on a Blind Date," DatingAdvice.com, August 6, 2022.
30. Elaine Hatfield, John T. Cacioppo, and Richard L. Rapson, "Emotional Contagion," **Current Directions in Psychological Science** 2, no. 3 (1993): 96–9.
31. James H. Fowler and Nicholas A. Christakis, "Dynamic Spread of Happiness in a Large Social Network: Longitudinal Analysis over 20 Years in the Framingham Heart Study," **BMJ** 337 (2008): a2338.
32. Alison L. Hill, David G. Rand, Martin A. Nowak, and Nicholas A. Christakis, "Emotions as Infectious Diseases in a Large Social Network: The SISa Model," **Proceedings of the Royal Society B: Biological Sciences** 277, no. 1701 (2010): 3827–35.
33. Elaine Hatfield, Lisamarie Bensman, Paul D. Thornton, and Richard L. Rapson, "New Perspectives on Emotional Contagion: A Review of Classic and Recent Research on Facial Mimicry and Contagion," **Interpersona: An International Journal on Personal Relationships** 8, no. 2 (2014): 159–79.
34. Bruno Wicker, Christian Keysers, Jane Plailly,

Jean-Pierre Royet, Vittorio Gallese, and Giacomo Rizzolatti, "Both of Us Disgusted in My Insula: The Common Neural Basis of Seeing and Feeling Disgust," **Neuron** 40, no. 3 (2003): 655–64.

35. India Morrison, Donna Lloyd, Giuseppe Di Pellegrino, and Neil Roberts, "Vicarious Responses to Pain in Anterior Cingulate Cortex: Is Empathy a Multisensory Issue?" **Cognitive, Affective, & Behavioral Neuroscience** 4, no. 2 (2004): 270–8.
36. Mary J. Howes, Jack E. Hokanson, and David A. Loewenstein, "Induction of Depressive Affect after Prolonged Exposure to a Mildly Depressed Individual," **Journal of Personality and Social Psychology** 49, no. 4 (1985): 1110–3.
37. Robert J. Littman and Maxwell L. Littman, "Galen and the Antonine Plague," **American Journal of Philology** 94, no. 3 (1973): 243–55.
38. Cassius Dio, "Book of Roman History," in **Loeb Classical Library** 9, trans. Earnest Cary and Herbert Baldwin Faoster (Cambridge, MA: Harvard University Press, 1925), 100–101.
39. Marcus Aurelius, "Marcus Aurelius," in **Loeb Classical Library** 58, ed. and trans. C. R. Haines (Cambridge, MA: Harvard University Press, 1916), 234–35.
40. Courtney Waite Miller and Michael E. Roloff, "When Hurt Continues: Taking Conflict Personally Leads to Rumination, Residual Hurt and Negative Motivations toward Someone Who Hurt Us," **Communication Quarterly** 62, no. 2 (2014): 193–213.
41. Denise C. Marigold, Justin V. Cavallo, John G.

Holmes, and Joanne V. Wood, "You Can't Always Give What You Want: The Challenge of Providing Social Support to Low Self-Esteem Individuals," **Journal of Personality and Social Psychology** 107, no. 1 (2014): 56–80.

42. Hao Shen, Aparna Labroo, and Robert S. Wyer Jr., "So Difficult to Smile: Why Unhappy People Avoid Enjoyable Activities," **Journal of Personality and Social Psychology** 119, no. 1 (2020): 23.
43. Robert M. Pirsig, **Zen and the Art of Motorcycle Maintenance: An Inquiry into Values** (New York: Random House, 1999).
44. Pavica Sheldon and Mary Grace Antony, "Forgive and Forget: A Typology of Transgressions and Forgiveness Strategies in Married and Dating Relationships," **Western Journal of Communication** 83, no. 2 (2019): 232–51.
45. Vincent R. Waldron and Douglas L. Kelley, "Forgiving Communication as a Response to Relational Transgressions," **Journal of Social and Personal Relationships** 22, no. 6 (2005): 723–42.
46. Sheldon and Antony, "Forgive and Forget."
47. Buddhaghosa Himi, **Visuddhimagga: The Path of Purification,** trans. Bhikkhu Ñāṇamoli (Sri Lanka: Buddhist Publication Society, 2010), 297.
48. Everett L. Worthington Jr., Charlotte Van Oyen Witvliet, Pietro Pietrini, and Andrea J. Miller, "Forgiveness, Health, and Well-being: A Review of Evidence for Emotional versus Decisional Forgiveness, Dispositional Forgivingness, and Reduced Unforgiveness," **Journal of Behavioral Medicine** 30, no. 4 (2007): 291–302.

49. Brad Blanton, **Radical Honesty** (New York: Random House, 1996).
50. Edel Ennis, Aldert Vrij, and Claire Chance, "Individual Differences and Lying in Everyday Life," **Journal of Social and Personal Relationships** 25, no. 1 (2008): 105–18.
51. Leon F. Seltzer, "The Narcissist's Dilemma: They Can Dish It Out, but . . ." **Psychology Today,** October 12, 2011.

Chapter Six: Friendship That Is Deeply Real

This chapter adapts ideas and takes passages from the following essays and podcast:

Arthur C. Brooks, "Sedentary Pandemic Life Is Bad for Our Happiness," How to Build a Life, **The Atlantic,** November 19, 2020; Arthur C. Brooks, "The Type of Love That Makes People Happiest," How to Build a Life, **The Atlantic,** February 11, 2021; Arthur C. Brooks, "The Hidden Toll of Remote Work," How to Build a Life, **The Atlantic,** April 1, 2021; Arthur C. Brooks, "The Best Friends Can Do Nothing for You," How to Build a Life, **The Atlantic,** April 8, 2021; Arthur C. Brooks, "What Introverts and Extroverts Can Learn from Each Other," How to Build a Life, **The Atlantic,** May 20, 2021; Arthur C. Brooks, "Which Pet Will Make You Happiest?" How to Build a Life, **The Atlantic,** August 5, 2021; Arthur C. Brooks, "Stop Waiting for Your Soul Mate," How to Build a Life, **The Atlantic,** September 9, 2021; Arthur C. Brooks, "Don't Surround Yourself with Admirers," How to Build a

Life, **The Atlantic,** June 30, 2022; Arthur C. Brooks, "Technology Can Make Your Relationships Shallower," How to Build a Life, **The Atlantic,** September 29, 2022; Arthur C. Brooks, "Marriage Is a Team Sport," How to Build a Life, **The Atlantic,** November 10, 2022; Arthur C. Brooks, "How We Learned to Be Lonely," How to Build a Life, **The Atlantic,** January 5, 2023; Arthur Brooks, "Love in the Time of Corona," **The Art of Happiness with Arthur Brooks,** podcast audio, 39:24, April 13, 2020.

1. Edgar Allan Poe, **The Complete Poetical Works of Edgar Allan Poe Including Essays on Poetry,** ed. John Henry Ingram (New York: A. L. Burt), published online by Project Gutenberg.
2. Ludwig, "Death of Edgar A Poe," **Richmond Enquirer,** October 16, 1849.
3. Edgar Allan Poe and Eugene Lemoine Didier, **Life and Poems** (New York: W. J. Widdleton, 1879), 101.
4. Melıkşah Demır, Ayça Özen, Aysun Doğan, Nicholas A. Bilyk, and Fanita A. Tyrell, "I Matter to My Friend, Therefore I Am Happy: Friendship, Mattering, and Happiness," **Journal of Happiness Studies** 12, no. 6 (2011): 983–1005.
5. Melıkşah Demır and Lesley A. Weitekamp, "I Am So Happy 'Cause Today I Found My Friend: Friendship and Personality as Predictors of Happiness," **Journal of Happiness Studies** 8, no. 2 (2007): 181–211.
6. Daniel A. Cox, "The State of American Friendship: Change, Challenges, and Loss," Survey Center on American Life, June 8, 2021.

7. Cox, "State of American Friendship."
8. John Whitesides, "From Disputes to a Breakup: Wounds Still Raw after U.S. Election," Reuters, February 7, 2017.
9. KFF, "As the COVID-19 Pandemic Enters the Third Year Most Adults Say They Have Not Fully Returned to Pre-Pandemic 'Normal,'" news release, April 6, 2022.
10. Maddie Sharpe and Alison Spencer, "Many Americans Say They Have Shifted Their Priorities around Health and Social Activities during COVID-19," Pew Research Center, August 18, 2022.
11. Sarah Davis, "59% of U.S. Adults Find It Harder to Form Relationships since COVID-19, Survey Reveals—Here's How That Can Harm Your Health," **Forbes,** July 12, 2022.
12. Lewis R. Goldberg, "The Development of Markers for the Big-Five Factor Structure," **Psychological Assessment** 4, no. 1 (1992): 26–42.
13. C. G. Jung, **Psychologische Typen** (Zurich: Rascher & Cie., 1921).
14. Hans Jurgen Eysenck, "Intelligence Assessment: A Theoretical and Experimental Approach," in **The Measurement of Intelligence** (Heidelberg, London, and New York: Springer Dordrecht, 1973), 194–211.
15. Rachel L. C. Mitchell and Veena Kumari, "Hans Eysenck's Interface between the Brain and Personality: Modern Evidence on the Cognitive Neuroscience of Personality," **Personality and Individual Differences** 103 (2016): 74–81.

16. Mats B. Küssner, "Eysenck's Theory of Personality and the Role of Background Music in Cognitive Task Performance: A Mini-Review of Conflicting Findings and a New Perspective," **Frontiers in Psychology** 8 (2017): 1991.
17. Peter Hills and Michael Argyle, "Happiness, Introversion–Extraversion and Happy Introverts," **Personality and Individual Differences** 30, no. 4 (2001): 595–608.
18. Ralph R. Greenson, "On Enthusiasm," **Journal of the American Psychoanalytic Association** 10, no. 1 (1962): 3–21.
19. Barry M. Staw, "The Escalation of Commitment to a Course of Action," **Academy of Management Review** 6, no. 4 (1981): 577–87.
20. Daniel C. Feiler and Adam M. Kleinbaum, "Popularity, Similarity, and the Network Extraversion Bias," **Psychological Science** 26, no. 5 (2015): 593–603.
21. Yehudi A. Cohen, "Patterns of Friendship," in **Social Structure and Personality: A Casebook** (New York: Holt, Rinehart and Winston, 1961), 351–86.
22. OnePoll, "Evite: Difficulty Making Friends," 72Point, May 2019.
23. Yixin Chen and Thomas Hugh Feeley, "Social Support, Social Strain, Loneliness, and Well-being among Older Adults: An Analysis of the Health and Retirement Study," **Journal of Social and Personal Relationships** 31, no. 2 (2014): 141–61.
24. Laura L. Carstensen, Derek M. Isaacowitz, and Susan T. Charles, "Taking Time Seriously: A

Theory of Socioemotional Selectivity," **American Psychologist** 54, no. 3 (1999): 165–81.

25. Aristotle, **Nicomachean Ethics** VIII (London: Kegan Paul, Trench, Trübner, and Company, 1893), 1, 3.
26. Michael E. Porter and Nitin Nohria, "How CEOs Manage Time," **Harvard Business Review,** July–August 2018.
27. Derek Thompson, "Workism Is Making Americans Miserable," **The Atlantic,** February 24, 2019.
28. Galatians 4:9, NIV; Yair Kramer, "Transformational Moments in Group Psychotherapy" (PhD diss., Rutgers University Graduate School of Applied and Professional Psychology, 2012).
29. "Magandiya Sutta: To Magandiya," trans. Thanissaro Bhikkhu, Access to Insight, November 30, 2013.
30. Thích Nhất Hạnh, **Being Peace** (Berkeley, CA: Parallax Press, 2020), 91.
31. Neal Krause, Kenneth I. Pargament, Peter C. Hill, and Gail Ironson, "Humility, Stressful Life Events, and Psychological Well-being: Findings from the Landmark Spirituality and Health Survey," **Journal of Positive Psychology** 11, no. 5 (2016): 499–510.
32. Philip Schaff and Henry Wace, eds., **Nicene and Post-Nicene Fathers: Basil: Letters and Select Works,** vol. 8 (Peabody, MA: Hendrickson, 1995), 446.
33. Adam K. Fetterman and Kai Sassenberg, "The Reputational Consequences of Failed Replications and Wrongness Admission among Scientists," **PLoS One** 10, no. 12 (2015): e0143723.

34. "Doris Kearns Goodwin on Lincoln and His 'Team of Rivals,'" interview by Dave Davies, **Fresh Air,** NPR, November 8, 2005.
35. Brian J. Fogg, **Tiny Habits: The Small Changes That Change Everything** (Boston: Houghton Mifflin Harcourt, 2020).
36. Paul Samuelson and William Nordhaus, **Economics,** 19th ed. (New York: McGraw Hill, 2010), 1.
37. Zhiling Zou, Hongwen Song, Yuting Zhang, and Xiaochu Zhang, "Romantic Love vs. Drug Addiction May Inspire a New Treatment for Addiction," **Frontiers in Psychology** 7 (2016): 1436.
38. Helen E. Fisher, Arthur Aron, and Lucy L. Brown, "Romantic Love: A Mammalian Brain System for Mate Choice," **Philosophical Transactions of the Royal Society B: Biological Sciences** 361, no. 1476 (2006): 2173–86.
39. Antina de Boer, Erin M. van Buel, and G. J. Ter Horst, "Love Is More Than Just a Kiss: A Neurobiological Perspective on Love and Affection," **Neuroscience** 201 (2012): 114–24.
40. Katherine Wu, "Love, Actually: The Science behind Lust, Attraction, and Companionship," **Science in the News** (blog), Harvard University: The Graduate School of Arts and Sciences, February 14, 2017.
41. "Harvard Study of Adult Development," Massachusetts General Hospital and Harvard Medical School, www.adultdevelopmentstudy.org.
42. Roberts J. Waldinger and Marc S. Schulz, "What's Love Got to Do with It? Social Functioning, Perceived Health, and Daily Happiness in Married

Octogenarians," **Psychology and Aging** 25, no. 2 (2010): 422–31.

43. Jungsik Kim and Elaine Hatfield, "Love Types and Subjective Well-being: A Cross-Cultural Study," **Social Behavior and Personality: An International Journal** 32, no. 2 (2004): 173–82.
44. Kevin A. Johnson, "Unrealistic Portrayals of Sex, Love, and Romance in Popular Wedding Films," in **Critical Thinking about Sex, Love, and Romance in the Mass Media,** ed. Mary-Lou Galician and Debra L. Merskin (Oxford, UK: Routledge, 2007), 306.
45. Litsa Renée Tanner, Shelley A. Haddock, Toni Schindler Zimmerman, and Lori K. Lund, "Images of Couples and Families in Disney Feature-Length Animated Films," **American Journal of Family Therapy** 31, no. 5 (2003): 355–73.
46. Chris Segrin and Robin L. Nabi, "Does Television Viewing Cultivate Unrealistic Expectations about Marriage?" **Journal of Communication** 52, no. 2 (2002): 247–63.
47. Karolien Driesmans, Laura Vandenbosch, and Steven Eggermont, "True Love Lasts Forever: The Influence of a Popular Teenage Movie on Belgian Girls' Romantic Beliefs," **Journal of Children and Media** 10, no. 3 (2016): 304–20.
48. Florian Zsok, Matthias Haucke, Cornelia Y. De Wit, and Dick PH Barelds, "What Kind of Love Is Love at First Sight? An Empirical Investigation," **Personal Relationships** 24, no. 4 (2017): 869–85.
49. Bjarne M. Holmes, "In Search of My 'One and

Only': Romance-Oriented Media and Beliefs in Romantic Relationship Destiny," **Electronic Journal of Communication** 17, no. 3 (2007): 1–23.

50. Benjamin H. Seider, Gilad Hirschberger, Kristin L. Nelson, and Robert W. Levenson, "We Can Work It Out: Age Differences in Relational Pronouns, Physiology, and Behavior in Marital Conflict," **Psychology and Aging** 24, no. 3 (2009): 604–13.
51. Joe J. Gladstone, Emily N. Garbinsky, and Cassie Mogilner, "Pooling Finances and Relationship Satisfaction," **Journal of Personality and Social Psychology** 123, no. 6 (2022): 1293–314; Joe Pinsker, "Should Couples Merge Their Finances?" **The Atlantic,** April 20, 2022.
52. Emily N. Garbinsky and Joe J. Gladstone, "The Consumption Consequences of Couples Pooling Finances," **Journal of Consumer Psychology** 29, no. 3 (2019): 353–69.
53. Laura K. Guerrero, "Conflict Style Associations with Cooperativeness, Directness, and Relational Satisfaction: A Case for a Six-Style Typology," **Negotiation and Conflict Management Research** 13, no. 1 (2020): 24–43.
54. Rhaina Cohen, "The Secret to a Fight-Free Relationship," **The Atlantic,** September 13, 2021.
55. David G. Blanchflower and Andrew J. Oswald, "Money, Sex and Happiness: An Empirical Study," **Scandinavian Journal of Economics** 106, no. 3 (2004): 393–415.
56. Kira S. Birditt and Toni C. Antonucci, "Relationship

Quality Profiles and Well-being among Married Adults," **Journal of Family Psychology** 21, no. 4 (2007): 595–604.

57. World Bank, "Internet Users for the United States (ITNETUSERP2USA)," Federal Reserve Bank of St. Louis.
58. Robert Kraut, Michael Patterson, Vicki Lundmark, Sara Kiesler, Tridas Mukophadhyay, and William Scherlis, "Internet Paradox: A Social Technology That Reduces Social Involvement and Psychological Well-being?" **American Psychologist** 53, no. 9 (1998): 1017–31.
59. Minh Hao Nguyen, Minh Hao, Jonathan Gruber, Will Marler, Amanda Hunsaker, Jaelle Fuchs, and Eszter Hargittai, "Staying Connected While Physically Apart: Digital Communication When Face-to-Face Interactions Are Limited," **New Media & Society** 24, no. 9 (2022): 2046–67.
60. Martha Newson, Yi Zhao, Marwa El Zein, Justin Sulik, Guillaume Dezecache, Ophelia Deroy, and Bahar Tunçgenç, "Digital Contact Does Not Promote Wellbeing, but Face-to-Face Contact Does: A Cross-National Survey during the COVID-19 Pandemic," **New Media & Society** (2021).
61. Michael Kardas, Amit Kumar, and Nicholas Epley, "Overly Shallow? Miscalibrated Expectations Create a Barrier to Deeper Conversation," **Journal of Personality and Social Psychology** 122, no. 3 (2022): 367–98.
62. Sarah M. Coyne, Laura M. Padilla-Walker, and Hailey G. Holmgren, "A Six-Year Longitudinal

Study of Texting Trajectories during Adolescence," **Child Development** 89, no. 1 (2018): 58–65.

63. Katherine Schaeffer, "Most U.S. Teens Who Use Cellphones Do It to Pass Time, Connect with Others, Learn New Things," Pew Research Center, August 23, 2019; Bethany L. Blair, Anne C. Fletcher, and Erin R. Gaskin, "Cell Phone Decision Making: Adolescents' Perceptions of How and Why They Make the Choice to Text or Call," **Youth & Society** 47, no. 3 (2015): 395–411.
64. César G. Escobar-Viera, César G., Ariel Shensa, Nicholas D. Bowman, Jaime E. Sidani, Jennifer Knight, A. Everette James, and Brian A. Primack, "Passive and Active Social Media Use and Depressive Symptoms among United States Adults," **Cyberpsychology, Behavior, and Social Networking** 21, no. 7 (2018): 437–43; Soyeon Kim, Lindsay Favotto, Jillian Halladay, Li Wang, Michael H. Boyle, and Katholiki Georgiades, "Differential Associations between Passive and Active Forms of Screen Time and Adolescent Mood and Anxiety Disorders," **Social Psychiatry and Psychiatric Epidemiology** 55, no. 11 (2020): 1469–78.
65. David Nield, "Try Grayscale Mode to Curb Your Phone Addiction," **Wired,** December 1, 2019.
66. Monique M. H. Pollmann, Tyler J. Norman, and Erin E. Crockett, "A Daily-Diary Study on the Effects of Face-to-Face Communication, Texting, and Their Interplay on Understanding and Relationship Satisfaction," **Computers in Human Behavior Reports** 3 (2021): 100088.

Chapter Seven: Work That Is Love Made Visible

This chapter adapts ideas and takes passages from the following essays and podcasts:

Arthur C. Brooks, "Your Professional Decline Is Coming (Much) Sooner Than You Think," **The Atlantic,** July 2019; Arthur C. Brooks, "4 Rules for Identifying Your Life's Work," How to Build a Life, **The Atlantic,** May 21, 2020; Arthur C. Brooks, "Stop Keeping Score," How to Build a Life, **The Atlantic,** January 21, 2021; Arthur C. Brooks, "Go Ahead and Fail," How to Build a Life, **The Atlantic,** February 25, 2021; Arthur C. Brooks, "Here's 10,000 Hours. Don't Spend It All in One Place," How to Build a Life, **The Atlantic,** March 18, 2021; Arthur C. Brooks, "Are You Dreaming Too Big?" How to Build a Life, **The Atlantic,** March 25, 2021; Arthur C. Brooks, "The Hidden Toll of Remote Work," How to Build a Life, **The Atlantic,** April 1, 2021; Arthur C. Brooks, "The Best Friends Can Do Nothing for You," How to Build a Life, **The Atlantic,** April 8, 2021; Arthur C. Brooks, "The Link between Self-Reliance and Well-Being," How to Build a Life, **The Atlantic,** July 8, 2021; Arthur C. Brooks, "Plan Ahead. Don't Post," How to Build a Life, **The Atlantic,** June 24, 2021; Arthur C. Brooks, "The Secret to Happiness at Work," How to Build a Life, **The Atlantic,** September 2, 2021; Arthur C. Brooks, "A Profession Is Not a Personality," How to Build a Life, **The Atlantic,** September 30, 2021; Arthur C. Brooks, "The Hidden Link between Workaholism and Mental Health," How to Build a

Life, **The Atlantic,** February 2, 2023; Rebecca Rashid and Arthur C. Brooks, "When Virtues Become Vices," interview with Anna Lembke, **How to Build a Happy Life,** podcast audio, 32:50, October 9, 2022; Rebecca Rashid and Arthur C. Brooks, "How to Spend Time on What You Value," interview with Ashley Whillans, **How to Build a Happy Life,** podcast audio, 34:24, October 23, 2022.

1. Timothy A. Judge and Shinichiro Watanabe, "Another Look at the Job Satisfaction–Life Satisfaction Relationship," **Journal of Applied Psychology** 78, no. 6 (1993): 939–48; Robert W. Rice, Janet P. Near, and Raymond G. Hunt, "The Job-Satisfaction/Life-Satisfaction Relationship: A Review of Empirical Research," **Basic and Applied Social Psychology** 1, no. 1 (1980): 37–64; Jeffrey S. Rain, Irving M. Lane, and Dirk D. Steiner, "A Current Look at the Job Satisfaction/ Life Satisfaction Relationship: Review and Future Considerations," **Human Relations** 44, no. 3 (1991): 287–307.
2. Kahlil Gibran, "On Work," in **The Prophet** (New York: Alfred A. Knopf, 1923).
3. CareerBliss Team, "The CareerBliss Happiest 2021," CareerBliss, January 6, 2021.
4. Kimberly Black, "Job Satisfaction Survey: What Workers Want in 2022," **Virtual Vocations** (blog), February 21, 2022.
5. Michael Davern, Rene Bautista, Jeremy Freese, Stephen L. Morgan, and Tom W. Smith, General Social Surveys, 1972–2021 Cross-section, NORC,

University of Chicago, 2018, gssdataexplorer.norc .org.

6. David G. Blanchflower, David N. F. Bell, Alberto Montagnoli, and Mirko Moro, "The Happiness Trade-off between Unemployment and Inflation," **Journal of Money, Credit and Banking** 46, no. S2 (2014): 117–41.
7. Mark R. Lepper, David Greene, and Richard E. Nisbett, "Undermining Children's Intrinsic Interest with Extrinsic Reward: A Test of the 'Overjustification' Hypothesis," **Journal of Personality and Social Psychology** 28, no. 1 (1973): 129–37.
8. Edward L. Deci, Richard Koestner, and Richard M. Ryan, "A Meta-analytic Review of Experiments Examining the Effects of Extrinsic Rewards on Intrinsic Motivation," **Psychological Bulletin** 125, no. 6 (1999): 627–68.
9. Jeannette L. Nolen, "Learned Helplessness," **Britannica,** last modified February 11, 2023.
10. Melissa Madeson, "Seligman's PERMA+ Model Explained: A Theory of Wellbeing," PositivePsychology.com, February 24, 2017; Esther T. Canrinus, Michelle Helms-Lorenz, Douwe Beijaard, Jaap Buitink, and Adriaan Hofman, "Self-Efficacy, Job Satisfaction, Motivation and Commitment: Exploring the Relationships between Indicators of Teachers' Professional Identity," **European Journal of Psychology of Education** 27, no. 1 (2012): 115–32.
11. Arthur C. Brooks, **Gross National Happiness: Why Happiness Matters for America—and How**

We Can Get More of It (New York: Basic Books, April 22, 2008).

12. Philip Muller, "Por Qué Me Gusta Ser Camarero Habiendo Estudiado Filosofía," **El Comidista,** October 22, 2018. This author was a graduate student of Arthur's.
13. Ting Ren, "Value Congruence as a Source of Intrinsic Motivation," **Kyklos** 63, no. 1 (2010): 94–109.
14. Ali Ravari, Shahrzad Bazargan-Hejazi, Abbas Ebadi, Tayebeh Mirzaei, and Khodayar Oshvandi, "Work Values and Job Satisfaction: A Qualitative Study of Iranian Nurses," **Nursing Ethics** 20, no. 4 (2013): 448–58.
15. Mary Ann von Glinow, Michael J. Driver, Kenneth Brousseau, and J. Bruce Prince, "The Design of a Career Oriented Human Resource System," **Academy of Management Review** 8, no. 1 (1983): 23–32.
16. "The Books of Sir Winston Churchill," International Churchill Society, October 17, 2008.
17. Charles McMoran Wilson, 1st Baron Moran, **Winston Churchill: The Struggle for Survival, 1940–1965** (London: Sphere Books, 1968), 167.
18. Anthony Storr, **Churchill's Black Dog, Kafka's Mice, and Other Phenomena of the Human Mind** (London: Fontana, 1990).
19. Sarah Turner, Natalie Mota, James Bolton, and Jitender Sareen, "Self-Medication with Alcohol or Drugs for Mood and Anxiety Disorders: A Narrative Review of the Epidemiological Literature," **Depression and Anxiety** 35, no. 9 (2018): 851–60.

20. Rosa M. Crum, Lareina La Flair, Carla L. Storr, Kerry M. Green, Elizabeth A. Stuart, Anika A. H. Alvanzo, Samuel Lazareck, James M. Bolton, Jennifer Robinson, Jitender Sareen, and Ramin Mojtabai, "Reports of Drinking to Self-Medicate Anxiety Symptoms: Longitudinal Assessment for Subgroups of Individuals with Alcohol Dependence," **Depression and Anxiety** 30, no. 2 (2013): 174–83.
21. Malissa A. Clark, Jesse S. Michel, Ludmila Zhdanova, Shuang Y. Pui, and Boris B. Baltes, "All Work and No Play? A Meta-analytic Examination of the Correlates and Outcomes of Workaholism," **Journal of Management** 42, no. 7 (2016): 1836–73; Satoshi Akutsu, Fumiaki Katsumura, and Shohei Yamamoto, "The Antecedents and Consequences of Workaholism: Findings from the Modern Japanese Labor Market," **Frontiers in Psychology** 13 (2022).
22. Lauren Spark, "Helping a Workaholic in Therapy: 18 Symptoms & Interventions," PositivePsychology.com, July 1, 2021.
23. Cecilie Schou Andreassen, Mark D. Griffiths, Rajita Sinha, Jørn Hetland, and Ståle Pallesen, "The Relationships between Workaholism and Symptoms of Psychiatric Disorders: A Large-Scale Cross-sectional Study," **PLoS One** 11, no. 5 (2016): e0152978.
24. Longqi Yang, David Holtz, Sonia Jaffe, Siddharth Suri, Shilpi Sinha, Jeffrey Weston, Connor Joyce, "The Effects of Remote Work on Collaboration

among Information Workers," **Nature Human Behaviour** 6, no. 1 (2022): 43–54.

25. National Center for Health Statistics, "Anxiety and Depression: Household Pulse Survey," Centers for Disease Control and Prevention, www.cdc.gov/nchs/covid19/pulse/mental-health.htm.
26. Rashid and Brooks, "When Virtues Become Vices."
27. Clark et al., "All Work and No Play?"
28. Rashid and Brooks, "How to Spend Time."
29. Andreassen et al., "Relationships between Workaholism."
30. Carly Schwickert, "The Effects of Objectifying Statements on Women's Self Esteem, Mood, and Body Image" (bachelor's thesis, Carroll College, 2015).
31. Evangelia (Lina) Papadaki, "Feminist Perspectives on Objectification," Stanford Encyclopedia of Philosophy, December 16, 2019.
32. Lola Crone, Lionel Brunel, and Laurent Auzoult, "Validation of a Perception of Objectification in the Workplace Short Scale (POWS)," **Frontiers in Psychology** 12 (2021): 651071.
33. Dmitry Tumin, Siqi Han, and Zhenchao Qian, "Estimates and Meanings of Marital Separation," **Journal of Marriage and Family** 77, no. 1 (2015): 312–22.
34. Margaret Diddams, Lisa Klein Surdyk, and Denise Daniels, "Rediscovering Models of Sabbath Keeping: Implications for Psychological Well-being," **Journal of Psychology and Theology** 32, no. 1 (2004): 3–11.

35. Lauren Grunebaum, "Dreaming of Being Special," **Psychology Today,** May 16, 2011.
36. Arthur C. Brooks, "'Success Addicts' Choose Being Special over Being Happy," How to Build a Life, **The Atlantic,** July 30, 2020.
37. Josemaría Escrivá, **In Love with the Church** (Strongsville, OH: Scepter, 2017), 78.

Chapter Eight: Find Your Amazing Grace

This chapter adapts ideas and takes passages from the following essays:

Arthur C. Brooks, "How to Navigate a Midlife Change of Faith," How to Build a Life, **The Atlantic,** August 13, 2020; Arthur C. Brooks, "The Subtle Mindset Shift That Could Radically Change the Way You See the World," How to Build a Life, **The Atlantic,** February 4, 2021; Arthur C. Brooks, "The Meaning of Life Is Surprisingly Simple," How to Build a Life, **The Atlantic,** October 21, 2021; Arthur C. Brooks, "Don't Objectify Yourself," How to Build a Life, **The Atlantic,** September 22, 2022; Arthur C. Brooks, "Mindfulness Hurts. That's Why It Works," How to Build a Life, **The Atlantic,** May 19, 2022; Arthur C. Brooks, "To Get Out of Your Head, Get Out of Your House," How to Build a Life, **The Atlantic,** August 11, 2022; Arthur C. Brooks, "How to Make Life More Transcendent," How to Build a Life, **The Atlantic,** October 27, 2022; Arthur C. Brooks, "How Thich Nhat Hanh Taught the West about Mindfulness," **Washington Post,** January 22, 2022; Rebecca Rashid and Arthur C.

Brooks, "How to Be Self-Aware," interview with Dan Harris, **How to Build a Happy Life,** podcast audio, 36:22, October 5, 2021; Rebecca Rashid and Arthur C. Brooks, interview with Ellen Langer, "How to Know That You Know Nothing," **How to Build a Happy Life,** podcast audio, 37:45, October 26, 2021.

1. Cary O'Dell, "'Amazing Grace'—Judy Collins (1970)," Library of Congress, www.loc.gov/static/programs/national-recording-preservation-board/documents/AmazingGrace.pdf.
2. Steve Turner, **Amazing Grace: The Story of America's Most Beloved Song** (New York: HarperCollins, 2009); "The Creation of 'Amazing Grace,'" Library of Congress, www.loc.gov/item/ihas.200149085.
3. Lisa Miller, Iris M. Balodis, Clayton H. McClintock, Jiansong Xu, Cheryl M. Lacadie, Rajita Sinha, and Marc N. Potenza, "Neural Correlates of Personalized Spiritual Experiences," **Cerebral Cortex** 29, no. 6 (2019): 2331–8.
4. Michael A. Ferguson, Frederic L. W. V. J. Schaper, Alexander Cohen, Shan Siddiqi, Sarah M. Merrill, Jared A. Nielsen, Jordan Grafman, Cosimo Urgesi, Franco Fabbro, and Michael D. Fox, "A Neural Circuit for Spirituality and Religiosity Derived from Patients with Brain Lesions," **Biological Psychiatry** 91, no. 4 (2022): 380–8.
5. Mario Beauregard and Vincent Paquette, "EEG Activity in Carmelite Nuns during a Mystical Experience," **Neuroscience Letters** 444, no. 1 (2008): 1–4.

6. Masaki Nishida, Nobuhide Hirai, Fumikazu Miwakeichi, Taketoshi Maehara, Kensuke Kawai, Hiroyuki Shimizu, and Sunao Uchida, "Theta Oscillation in the Human Anterior Cingulate Cortex during All-Night Sleep: An Electrocorticographic Study," **Neuroscience Research** 50, no. 3 (2004): 331–41.
7. Andrew A. Abeyta and Clay Routledge, "The Need for Meaning and Religiosity: An Individual Differences Approach to Assessing Existential Needs and the Relation with Religious Commitment, Beliefs, and Experiences," **Personality and Individual Differences** 123 (2018): 6–13.
8. Lisa Miller, Priya Wickramaratne, Marc J. Gameroff, Mia Sage, Craig E. Tenke, and Myrna M. Weissman, "Religiosity and Major Depression in Adults at High Risk: A Ten-Year Prospective Study," **American Journal of Psychiatry** 169, no. 1 (2012): 89–94; Michael Inzlicht and Alexa M. Tullett, "Reflecting on God: Religious Primes Can Reduce Neurophysiological Response to Errors," **Psychological Science** 21, no. 8 (2010): 1184–90.
9. Tracy A. Balboni, Tyler J. VanderWeele, Stephanie D. Doan-Soares, Katelyn N. G. Long, Betty R. Ferrell, George Fitchett, and Harold G. Koenig, "Spirituality in Serious Illness and Health," **JAMA** 328, no. 2 (2022): 184–97.
10. Jesse Graham and Jonathan Haidt, "Beyond Beliefs: Religions Bind Individuals into Moral Communities," **Personality and Social Psychology Review** 14, no. 1 (2010): 140–50.
11. Monica L. Gallegos and Chris Segrin, "Exploring

the Mediating Role of Loneliness in the Relationship between Spirituality and Health: Implications for the Latino Health Paradox," **Psychology of Religion and Spirituality** 11, no. 3 (2019): 308–18.

12. Thích Nhất Hạnh, **The Miracle of Mindfulness: An Introduction to the Practice of Meditation** (Boston: Beacon Press, 1996), 6.
13. Kendra Cherry, "Benefits of Mindfulness," VeryWell Mind, September 2, 2022.
14. Michael D. Mrazek, Michael S. Franklin, Dawa Tarchin Phillips, Benjamin Baird, and Jonathan W. Schooler, "Mindfulness Training Improves Working Memory Capacity and GRE Performance While Reducing Mind Wandering," **Psychological Science** 24, no. 5 (2013): 776–81.
15. Martin E. P. Seligman, Peter Railton, Roy F. Baumeister, and Chandra Sripada, **Homo Prospectus** (Oxford, UK: Oxford University Press, 2016).
16. Jonathan Smallwood, Annamay Fitzgerald, Lynden K. Miles, and Louise H. Phillips, "Shifting Moods, Wandering Minds: Negative Moods Lead the Mind to Wander," **Emotion** 9, no. 2 (2009): 271–6.
17. Kyle Cease, **I Hope I Screw This Up: How Falling in Love with Your Fears Can Change the World** (New York: Simon & Schuster, 2017); Tiago Figueiredo, Gabriel Lima, Pilar Erthal, Rafael Martins, Priscila Corção, Marcelo Leonel, Vanessa Ayrão, Dídia Fortes, and Paulo Mattos, "Mind-Wandering, Depression, Anxiety and ADHD: Disentangling the Relationship,"

Psychiatry Research 285 (2020): 112798; Miguel Ibaceta and Hector P. Madrid, "Personality and Mind-Wandering Self-Perception: The Role of Meta-Awareness," **Frontiers in Psychology** 12 (2021): 581129; Shane W. Bench and Heather C. Lench, "On the Function of Boredom," **Behavioral Sciences** 3, no. 3 (2013): 459–72.

18. Neda Sedighimornani, "Is Shame Managed through Mind-Wandering?" **Europe's Journal of Psychology** 15, no. 4 (2019): 717–32.
19. Smallwood et al., "Shifting Moods."
20. Heidi A. Wayment, Ann F. Collier, Melissa Birkett, Tinna Traustadóttir, and Robert E. Till, "Brief Quiet Ego Contemplation Reduces Oxidative Stress and Mind-Wandering," **Frontiers in Psychology** 6 (2015): 1481.
21. Hạnh, **Miracle of Mindfulness;** Anonymous 19th Century Russian Peasant, **The Way of a Pilgrim and The Pilgrim Continues on His Way: Collector's Edition** (Magdalene Press, 2019).
22. Lauren A. Leotti, Sheena S. Iyengar, and Kevin N. Ochsner, "Born to Choose: The Origins and Value of the Need for Control," **Trends in Cognitive Sciences** 14, no. 10 (2010): 457–63; Amitai Shenhav, David G. Rand, and Joshua D. Greene, "Divine Intuition: Cognitive Style Influences Belief in God," **Journal of Experimental Psychology: General** 141, no. 3 (2012): 423–8.
23. Mary Kekatos, "The Rise of the 'Indoor Generation': A Quarter of Americans Spend Almost All Day Inside, New Figures Reveal," **DailyMail.com,** May 15, 2018.

24. Outdoor Foundation, **2019 Outdoor Participation Report,** Outdoor Industry Association, 2020.
25. "Global Survey Finds We're Lacking Fresh Air and Natural Light, as We Spend Less Time in Nature," Velux Media Centre, May 21, 2019.
26. Wendell Cox Consultancy, "US Urban and Rural Population: 1800–2000," Demographia.
27. Howard Frumkin, Gregory N. Bratman, Sara Jo Breslow, Bobby Cochran, Peter H. Kahn Jr., Joshua J. Lawler, and Phillip S. Levin, "Nature Contact and Human Health: A Research Agenda," **Environmental Health Perspectives** 125, no. 7 (2017): 075001; Nielsen, **The Nielsen Total Audience Report: Q1 2016** (New York: Nielsen Company, 2016).
28. Gregory N. Bratman, Gretchen C. Daily, Benjamin J. Levy, and James J. Gross, "The Benefits of Nature Experience: Improved Affect and Cognition," **Landscape and Urban Planning** 138 (2015): 41–50.
29. F. Stephan Mayer, Cynthia McPherson Frantz, Emma Bruehlman-Senecal, and Kyffin Dolliver, "Why Is Nature Beneficial? The Role of Connectedness to Nature," **Environment and Behavior** 41, no. 5 (2009): 607–43.
30. Henry David Thoreau, "Walking," **The Atlantic,** June 1862.
31. Adam Alter, "How Nature Resets Our Minds and Bodies," **The Atlantic,** March 29, 2013.
32. Kenneth P. Wright Jr., Andrew W. McHill, Brian R. Birks, Brandon R. Griffin, Thomas Rusterholz, and Evan D. Chinoy, "Entrainment of the Human

Circadian Clock to the Natural Light-Dark Cycle," **Current Biology** 23, no. 16 (2013): 1554–8.

33. Wendy Menigoz, Tracy T. Latz, Robin A. Ely, Cimone Kamei, Gregory Melvin, and Drew Sinatra, "Integrative and Lifestyle Medicine Strategies Should Include Earthing (Grounding): Review of Research Evidence and Clinical Observations," **Explore** 16, no. 3 (2020): 152–160.
34. This is based on a conversation with Arthur.
35. C. S. Lewis, **Mere Christianity** (London: Geoffrey Bles, 1952).

Conclusion: Now, Become the Teacher

This chapter adapts ideas and takes passages from the following essay:

Arthur C. Brooks, "The Kind of Smarts You Don't Find in Young People," How to Build a Life, **The Atlantic,** March 3, 2022.

1. Safiye Temel Aslan, "Is Learning by Teaching Effective in Gaining 21st Century Skills? The Views of Pre-Service Science Teachers," **Educational Sciences: Theory & Practice** 15, no. 6 (2015).
2. John A. Bargh and Yaacov Schul, "On the Cognitive Benefits of Teaching," **Journal of Educational Psychology** 72, no. 5 (1980): 593–604.
3. Richard E. Brown, "Hebb and Cattell: The Genesis of the Theory of Fluid and Crystallized Intelligence," **Frontiers in Human Neuroscience** 10 (2016): 606; Alan S. Kaufman, Cheryl K. Johnson, and Xin Liu, "A CHC Theory-Based Analysis of Age Differences

on Cognitive Abilities and Academic Skills at Ages 22 to 90 Years," **Journal of Psychoeducational Assessment** 26, no. 4 (2008): 350–81; Arthur C. Brooks, **From Strength to Strength: Finding Success, Happiness, and Deep Purpose in the Second Half of Life** (New York: Portfolio, 2022).

4. Martin Luther King Jr., "Loving Your Enemies" (sermon, Dexter Avenue Baptist Church, Montgomery, AL, November 17, 1957).

About the Authors

ARTHUR C. BROOKS is the Parker Gilbert Montgomery Professor at Harvard Kennedy School and professor of management practice at Harvard Business School, where he teaches courses on happiness. He is the creator of the popular How to Build a Life column at **The Atlantic,** an acclaimed public speaker, and the author of bestselling books, including **From Strength to Strength** and **Love Your Enemies.**

As a global media leader and communications pioneer, **OPRAH WINFREY** has built unparalleled connections with people around the world. Through **The Oprah Winfrey Show,** she entertained, enlightened, and uplifted millions of viewers for twenty-five years. Her accomplishments as a philanthropist and her commitment to books, reading, and education have established her as one of the most respected and admired public figures today.